Praise for *Balan*

"I am a firm believer that one of the ~~most effective~~ ... for every student is a healthy adult. If you have any desire to make an impact in your role as an educator and to do so in a way that is sustainable, you owe it to yourself to read *Balance Like a Pirate*. Jessica Cabeen, Jessica Johnson, and Sarah Johnson draw from rich personal experience to lay out a practical roadmap to sustainability through the Four Quadrants of Balance."

—**Adam L. Saenz**, PhD, DMin, psychologist, consultant, author of *The Power of a Teacher*

"For years, educators have struggled with the demands of the job trying to be everything to everyone, often resulting in unproductive guilt. In *Balance Like a Pirate*, authors Jessica Cabeen, Jessica Johnson, and Sarah Johnson honor our diverse roles as a teacher, principal, parent, friend, wife and husband, etc. The book is filled with ideas, personal stories, practical experiences, and thoughts for honoring our unique situations throughout various points in our work, giving us permission to take care of ourselves first. Pause, take a deep breath, and allow yourself to ease into this book to refresh your mind and soul so you can bring your best to every role."

—**Jimmy Casas**, educator, speaker, author of *CULTURIZE*

"In *Balance Like a Pirate*, Jessica Cabeen, Jessica Johnson, and Sarah Johnson give phenomenal insight to navigating the busy demands of the life of an educator. They share practical, easy to implement strategies along with a big dose of inspiration and motivation. I highly recommend this book and know that I will reference it often in the years ahead."

—**Beth Houf**, proud principal of Fulton Middle School, coauthor of *Lead Like a PIRATE*

"*Balance Like a Pirate* is one of the most refreshing books I've read in a long time. This message is always important, but in our 24/7 lives and careers, it's more important than ever. Cabeen, Johnson, and Johnson do a wonderful job 'balancing' practical information with their own personal stories. They really draw you into the book, and the practical advice already has me thinking about my own balancing act. All three of these authors do a wonderful job of helping the reader to analyze their own life, to see where a change can be made, and to always remember that our professional learning network is vital to help us through those hard times. *Balance Like a Pirate* is a must read!"

—**Adam Welcome**, educator, author, speaker, marathoner

"*Balance Like a Pirate* is a must read for all educators. Deeply rooted in research-based methods and mindfulness practices, these incredible leaders provide honest, real-life examples with practical solutions that can be implemented immediately to help even the most burnt-out educators rediscover their passion while living their best life. *Balance Like a Pirate* won't just change your mindset, it will change your life."

—**Ashley Denisen,** @ashley_denisen, educator, Minnesota

"*Balance Like a Pirate* is an important book for all educators—professionals who too often are overworked and overstressed. This book moves beyond platitudes and, instead, offers keen insights, resources, personal stories, and action steps for moving beyond 'work-life' balance and simply doing a better job at 'life-balance.' This book is written by three highly respected educators who share their own struggles with balancing personal, professional, passion, and positional responsibilities as well as their solutions for overcoming such struggles. If you serve as an educator in any role, you must read this book. It will resonate with you and rejuvenate you. Get ready to 'set sail' on a journey you will not soon forget and which you will want to return to often as a way to serve your students, colleagues, friends, and family members more passionately."

—**Jeffrey Zoul**, EdD, author, speaker, leadership coach, and president of ConnectEDD

"*Balance Like a Pirate* is easy to read, relevant, and impactful! Being an educational professional and parent today is hard and often leads to burnout. Jessica Cabeen, Jessica Johnson, and Sarah Johnson challenge you to reflect on your practices and provide essential tips and tricks to find cohesion in the four main quadrants of your life. I will continually go back to *Balance Like a Pirate* when I need inspiration, motivation and ideas to find stability my own life."

—**Katie Keller**, instructional coach, Austin Public Schools, Austin Minnesota

"*Balance Like a Pirate* invites you on a journey to rediscover yourself as a person, as an educator, and as a leader. Jessica J., Jessica C., and Sarah share with great vulnerability and authenticity their personal narratives, challenges, and successes, to help others strengthen their practice, reflection, and to reclaim their lives in the continuing process of balancing work and life. They will engage you with enthusiasm and ignite your soul to keep following your dreams, to be present, and to never forget yourself in the process. In the continuing quest for balance, these amazing women, mothers, and leaders will capture your heart and passion for education, will remind you of your why, and will become your mentors to leading a happy and balanced life."

—**Roman Nowak**, teacher/student success leader/agent
of transformation, *CSDCEO*, Ontario, Canada

"There's no time like the present. *Balance Like a Pirate* is authentic and simply keeps it real. Whether you are struggling to find that work-life balance personally or professionally, whether you are now starting a journey, midway through it, or nearing the end of it, the stories shared are relatable to all. If you are finally ready to make a change and steer your ship in the right direction, get ready to set sail with *Balance Like a Pirate*. As you know, you must put on your oxygen mask first before you can save anyone else, so get ready to learn how to breathe."

—**Onica L. Mayers**, @O_L_Mayers, lead learner,
Principal of the Year 2017

"You. Need. This. Book. Trust me. As an elementary teacher, global keynote speaker, CEO of my own company, author, fitness fanatic, faith-filled Christian, dog mom, and proud auntie, *Balance Like a Pirate* resonated with me on so many levels. After reading this book, I've found the four balance quadrants (personal, professional, positional, and passions) to serve as a valuable guide in my efforts to fit it all in, focus in and do it well, reframe my day, and identify the true priorities and non-negotiables with my time. This book helped me reflect and reprioritize. What are you waiting for? If you're hoping to regain balance, let go of the things out of your control, and free up time and space for you, start reading now! You won't regret it."

—**Kayla Delzer**, globally awarded teacher,
author, CEO of Top Dog Teaching Inc.

"This is a book that offers hope! There are educators everywhere who are tired; they are burning the candle at both ends, and they feel like their soul is being sucked dry. In *Balance Like a Pirate*, Jessica Cabeen, Jessica Johnson, and Sarah Johnson provide a road map for teachers and administrators seeking to regain control of their lives. Through their raw vulnerability and poignant personal stories, these ladies provide a compelling approach to finding the balance that we all crave. These authors are 'real,' and that's one of the things I love about their writing. *Balance Like a Pirate* will resonate with every passionate educator."

—**Danny Steele**, award-winning principal, speaker, and writer

"In this always-on age, every educator is at risk of burnout. The authors of *Balance Like a Pirate* are no strangers to the tensions of being stretched too thin by personal and professional commitments. If you're reaching your limits, reach for *Balance Like a Pirate*. It's full of empathy, humor, and practical strategies to regain balance and have the life—and the impact—you want. But it's not just about balancing the personal and professional—you'll also learn specific strategies for clarifying your professional goals and passions, developing a plan for pursuing them, and building the resilience you'll need to overcome the inevitable setbacks. Jessica Cabeen, Jessica Johnson, and Sarah Johnson have created an approach to life as an educator that will save careers, help families, and impact the profession for generations to come. Highly recommended."

—**Justin Baeder,** PhD, director of The Principal Center
and author of *Now We're Talking!*

"In your hands is a real gem, a map, to guide you on your journey to attaining balance. My most popular coaching session tackles the issue of balance, and I'm excited to have another tool to use with leaders in order to understand and address balance. Burnout is very real; we cannot lead at our best unless we live at our best. This book will help you understand how to make that dream a reality."

—**Danny "Sunshine" Bauer**, host of the
Better Leaders Better Schools podcast

BALANCE

Like a PIRATE

Going Beyond Work-Life Balance to Ignite Passion and Thrive as an Educator

Jessica Cabeen   Jessica Johnson   Sarah Johnson

Balance Like a Pirate
© 2018 by Jessica Cabeen, Jessica Johnson, and Sarah Johnson

This book is available at special discounts when purchased in quantity for use as premiums, promotions, fundraisers, or for educational use. For inquiries and details, contact the publisher at books@daveburgessconsulting.com.

Published by Dave Burgess Consulting, Inc.
San Diego, CA
DaveBurgessConsulting.com

Cover Design by Genesis Kohler
Editing and Interior Design by My Writers' Connection

Library of Congress Control Number: 2018949175
Paperback ISBN: 978-1-946444-92-9
Ebook ISBN: 978-1-946444-94-3

First Printing: July 2018

This Book Is Dedicated to . . .

My grandmother, the woman who taught me the importance of being my best self and living life to the fullest.

—Jessica Cabeen

My husband, Craig, and my boys, Nathan and Alex, who have been patient with me while I worked on figuring out work-life balance. Through this journey, I've realized I can have quality family time and nurture my personal well-being and passions, while still pursuing excellence at work.

—Jessica Johnson

My daughters, Selene and Adelle, who have given me purpose to be the best version of myself at home; my husband, Joe, who has given me the grace to transform; my coauthors who have helped me realize my dreams of publishing a book; and my heavenly Father who graces my purpose to speak to this message.

—Sarah Johnson

Together, we would like to acknowledge our professional learning network, which includes too many colleagues to count. We have continued to grow professionally and personally through our connections on Twitter, as well as our extended conversations on Voxer. Together, we are better, in all quadrants of our lives!

CONTENTS

FOREWORD

Balance is an issue for many school leaders. How could it not be? We carry around smartphones, giving us immediate access to email and text. What was once a tool to make our lives easier, smartphones have become a way to make sure we can work all day—*and* all night too if we need to. Many of us even have notifications activated so they make sounds to tell us when we receive texts or messages. And we wonder why we have a balance problem?

So many different issues pull on leaders, and as we move from year to year, our jobs seem to get more complicated. According to the Organisation for Economic and Co-Operational Development:

- More and more tasks have been added to school leaders' workloads,
- Most of the leadership tasks are carried out by one individual; and
- Leaders are receiving insufficient preparation and training.

Leaders are charged with many responsibilities, and Robinson cites the following as the most important aspects of instructional leadership:

- Establishing goals and expectations
- Resourcing strategically
- Ensuring quality teaching
- Leading teacher learning and development
- Ensuring an orderly and safe environment

Although Robinson's responsibilities range in effect from .27 (low) to .84 (high), the level of effort involved in completing them is another reason we find ourselves with a balance issue.

The sad part about balance is the opportunity cost leadership creates. When we pursue responsibilities to increase our potential to be successful leaders, the opportunity cost usually begins at home. In our effort to be better leaders, we sometimes neglect our families or miss important events our children participate in because we are supporting other children who may not have parents who are involved at all. We miss dinners at night and soon find ourselves "catching up" on work during the weekends. We wear "going to the office on Sunday" as a badge of honor, but forget we have loved ones waiting for us at home.

Balance Like a PIRATE, by Jessica Cabeen, Jessica Johnson, and Sarah Johnson, is an important contribution to our discussions around leadership. We need to look at this book as a call to action for those of us with balance issues. This does not mean we need to neglect our jobs. But it does mean we need to neglect our personal lives *less*. Leadership is complicated and multifaceted and can put us at risk of psychological and physiological stress. We need to find new ways to approach our daily routines—and perhaps look to the pirates for some help!

While I'm not sure how pirates dealt with balance, I do know Jessica, Jessica, and Sarah understand the lives of leaders and the need for balance. I have been a big fan of each of them individually for quite some time. I'm excited to see them team up because each of them brings a unique perspective to the discussion around balance. Some of the experiences they share in the book were difficult and became their own catalysts to find personal balance.

Jessica, Jessica, and Sarah begin by writing about burnout. I travel a lot and work with many leaders in North America and abroad, and I have learned some of the greatest leaders who care the most are the ones most at risk of burning out. We need good leaders who can stay in the role for many years—because longevity matters. So sit back and take a deep breath. Find some time to read their words, learn from their experiences, and put their advice into action so you find the balance that you need as a leader.

—Peter DeWitt, EdD, author, consultant,
Finding Common Ground blog (Education Week)

THE BURNOUT FACTOR

Education is under fire more than ever before. Budget cuts and legislation, along with the public's perception of education, have changed significantly in the past five years. Every educator has likely felt unsupported, unappreciated, overworked, and underpaid at least one time in his or her career. With the heavy burden in the workplace, educators often arrive home, emotionally and physically exhausted, and then feel guilty for never having enough or being enough to fully engage at home.

We are three of those school leaders—torn between our passions for our job and our personal lives. We come from three different districts and three very different life circumstances. Initially Twitter brought us together to support and encourage other educators to *thrive*—not just survive—in this field of work. Via Twitter, Voxer, and our blogs, we have engaged in ongoing conversations around the topic of balance for years, sharing our personal struggles, *aha* moments, life hacks, and much more. We have learned so much from each other and our professional learning networks (PLN) that we are eager to pass everything on to you in *Balance Like a Pirate*.

We want this book to feel like a conversation as you read, which is why we share our personal stories. In some stories, we will identify ourselves, and some stories might be modified slightly and without identification because they're just too personal or connected to our schools to be confidentially disclosed. (You're an educator, so we know you get it.) Since two of us are "Jessica," Jessica Cabeen will remain "Jessica" and Jessica Johnson will be identified as "JJ." We're just going to ignore the fact two of us also share the surname Johnson!

JJ. I have a love-hate relationship with my job. I love the kids, I love the service, and I love the collaboration and teamwork of incredible teachers and support staff working together to create the best school possible. I love the supportive community and parents, and I love having an impact on the lives of so many students.

I love my job and feel it's the best job in the world. So why did I say I had a "love-*hate*" relationship with it? Because I hate that it can be so exhausting, time consuming, and emotionally and mentally challenging. And I hate that, at times, it requires me to put work before family and self. For many years I did just that: I let my passion for the work and my workaholic tendencies take over my life to the point I was completely out of balance. I wasn't paying much attention to my family or myself. ■

There has to be a better way.

We wanted to write this book because we *want* there to be a better way. Author Toni Morrison says, "If there's a book that you want to read, but it hasn't been written yet, then you must write it." So, while we are not experts at balance—we are educators in the field, trying to do good work and learning ways to find better balance—we are sharing our struggles with you because we know we are not alone. We know this struggle exists for all educators, and we wanted to provide a resource to prompt discussion and, hopefully, change.

Jessica. I took action to regain my balance after a massive wake-up call. I had been leading at the secondary level in a variety of positions for about five years. Our oldest son Kenny was in first grade, and our son Isaiah had recently joined our family as a five-and-a-half-year-old from Africa. While on adoption leave from my middle-school assistant principal position, I recognized how much I was missing by working—*all* the time.

Throughout my career, I had seen how advances in technology had enhanced learning and helped us become more efficient educators, but suddenly I realized that being connected 24/7 was a burden. I realized my phone was my best friend. I felt obligated to be "on" all the time, which meant I had little to no energy for the men in my life who called me "wife" and "mom." After that hard realization, I started making significant changes in my professional life—changes made a positive impact on my personal life as well. I may have missed out on some critical early years of my boys' lives, but by putting work and life into perspective and having others to help me stay accountable, I now have the opportunity to live my "titles" in order of true importance: wife, mother, leader. ■

Sarah. As a secondary-level leader, I have always struggled for balance. The heaviness of teen mental-health challenges, helping teachers motivate the unmotivated, and being present outside school hours on the fields, courts, and in the audience takes its toll. Combine this with heightened accountability for all students to succeed beyond high school while providing programming to meet all these individual needs on a tight budget, and balance feels nearly impossible.

Secondary-level leaders could spend every day—and evening—focused on their "title" responsibilities. I know I could. But where does this leave the other aspects of their lives? What about your own children who need you in their lives? What about your spouse, friends, and family? If you devote all your energy and time to your position, you fall into the trap of forgetting to learn and neglecting what lights you on fire besides being an educator. Many of my colleagues suffer in their personal lives, professional growth, and individual passions. Burnout is taking its toll.

I know this struggle firsthand. In recent years, my need for balance became evident when my marriage ended up almost shattering, I experienced major turmoil at work, and had to deal with the loss of a sibling. I felt like a shell of my former self. It was clear something had to change, and I am fortunate to have focused on intentionally transforming into a more balanced version of myself—thanks in large part to the reflective act of crafting this book. In fact, composing this work has been a labor of love, transforming all three of us. Even if we will never meet you, we truly believe the lessons we have learned and now share with you are life affirming and will transform you also.

I know from experience that secondary-level educators, especially, tend to be slow to collaborate, which stunts our growth and invites burnout. I've also learned that connection with and support and tips from other educators are crucial to developing balance. It has taken me years as a connected educator to find a crew of connected high-school leaders in the field. It's time to get off our islands and set sail together! Bring a friend or two along and let's work to create lives of balance! ■

Are You a Firefighter or a Fire Chief?

As teachers, we are constantly tasked with taking on more and more. As school leaders, it is hard to navigate when you should jump into action or support, encourage, and coach. Regardless, if you are a school leader or educator, the message is the same: If you overextend yourself or take on more than you should, you are at risk of changing roles—shifting from teacher to leader (or vice versa) or trying to do both simultaneously. Many of us burn out because we jump too far into the flames when we should be somewhere else. Delegation of authority can be hard to learn for a new administrator—or leaders of any kind of team or organization for that matter. But it is an important skill. Leaders who do not understand where their energy goes may be in danger of burning out. The same is true for teachers who spend excessive amounts of time on tasks with very little impact on student learning (or their own professional learning). Sometimes educators simply spread themselves too thin by volunteering for various committees. A colleague calls this the "Pavlov's Dog for Educators" Syndrome: Teachers hear a call for help, and they instantly raise a hand to volunteer.

Jessica. I'm fascinated with the television show *Chicago Fire.* The courage of the members of the 25th Battalion Chicago Fire Department and their loyalty to mission and calling is inspiring. I've watched the show for a while—amazed at the action and reaction of each person in crisis—but only during the past year have I seen the parallels between fire personnel and educators. Both have a deep sense of loyalty and dedication to their work. Firefighters and fire chiefs work together to protect the community via search and rescue efforts; educators and administrators work together to ensure all students have a safe, engaging environment in which to learn. ■

Firefighters provide hands-on, direct support to search and rescue efforts, while fire chiefs are responsible for the "hands-off" aspects of search and rescue, including hiring, training, supervision, and administration.

Similarly, teachers provide the hands-on, mission-driven focus to ensure every student learns to her optimal level while administrators are charged with supervision, setting the mission of the school, being the face and voice of the school, and removing any roadblocks so teachers can reach every student.

Knowing our role(s) is essential to maintain (or regain) balance in our lives and in our professions. Fire chiefs can't be going into the fires, and administrators can't be *every*thing for *every*one *all* the time.

On the other hand, if firefighters tried to accomplish their responsibilities and the job of fire chiefs—worrying about the next fiscal year, scheduling safety trainings for the entire unit, etc.—they would be significantly less effective at their primary job: saving lives. Likewise, teachers need dedicated time to plan, collaborate, and problem solve to meet the academic needs of their students. They *shouldn't* be distracted by figuring out lunch schedules, arranging transportation for field trips, and worrying if their immediate supervisor respects the work they do and is invested in their success.

JJ. I have learned I have to stop running into the fire. I am a fixer; I want to be first on the scene. Plus, I feel that if I am *busy*, I am doing what I am supposed to be doing. But by running into the fire first, I am actually preventing the highly trained and accomplished teacher from having the opportunity to shine and share his knowledge. Unintentionally running into fires first—creating behavior plans or the specific scope and sequence of a curriculum—takes those opportunities away from the ones who have the best expertise: the teachers. And who wants to correct the boss? ■

So teachers need to be allowed to do the job they were trained to do. But they don't need to take on the tasks of administrators. If teachers are overwhelmed with the "extra" workload and busyness of running a school, they won't have the time or mental space to do the work they were called and hired to do: teach.

Increasing expectations and demands placed on students, many times without increasing support from government leaders, have a direct impact on teachers and school leaders. We all are doing more with less, which means that, as leaders, we have to keep the *whole* person in mind. We have to stop looking at educators based only on their positions and their actions from 8:00 a.m. to 4:00 p.m. and find how we can support, encourage, and inspire everyone (ourselves included) to be better *for themselves* first so they can be better *for others*.

Although we want to embrace and share the message of "work-life balance," our goal for writing goes beyond simply wanting educators and school leaders to find balance. Universally, educators need to internalize the message of *Balance Like a Pirate*. Otherwise, burnout will prevail, and we will continue to lose passionate and talented educators.

The Balance Quadrants

Throughout this book, we will provide strategies and supports to lead at home and at school. We will weave in and out of the four quadrants of balance—*personal, professional, positional, passions*—much like life does. We created a visual to show balance isn't about fifty/fifty or eighty/twenty or any set combination of numbers, minutes in a day, or days in a week.

When we talk about *personal* balance, we are referencing everything that really makes you who you are—what are the "titles" outside of your job, and how do you cultivate them? Are you a runner, a mother, a spouse, an avid reader? How about someone who practices yoga, or takes care of a parent in the middle place of life? Whatever defines you is what we consider your personal quadrant.

Defining *positional* balance is all about our day job. Are you an educator, an administrator? Are you an aspiring educator or looking for a change of role/position? Whatever you do that earns income or provides you financial stability fits in the *position* category.

In education we know that we never, ever stop learning. *Professional* balance is just that—how are you continuing to learn, grow, and enhance your knowledge and understanding of your role? Learning is not just about going to class; this learning can come from books, blogs, podcasts, conferences—any way that you relate to and can increase your knowledge that impacts the school and students you serve—that is *professional* learning.

Your **passions** comprise the fourth quadrant. What are your sparks, what ignites your flame, what are you excited about . . . nervous for . . . or afraid to try because you know if you do you will love it? Creating a blog, playing in a band, painting, whatever it is that fills you completely up! I (Jessica) think of *passion* this way: I would do it for free. Our *passions* are the compass we need to keep our quadrants in balance, and to continue to find joy in this journey called life.

Here is a sample grid to give you perspective:

Personal	Professional
• Wellness in domains like physical, emotional, and financial • Mindfulness • Family and relationships	• Cultivating a Professional Learning Network (PLN) • Continuing your own learning • Going back to school, and setting your own course for ongoing learning
Positional	**Passions**
• Your specific role and duties • Time management • Dealing with difficult situations • Identifying priorities, and investing time and energy in these goals	• Your joys outside of your job—what lights you up as a person—and finding ways to stoke the embers and keep the fire burning

There are times when your focus needs to be on one quadrant more than the others, but for optimum effectiveness and your best life, you must not completely neglect any of these areas. We believe every educator can achieve balance by setting goals in the different domains in life and holding themselves accountable each week to accomplishing one thing in each area. You will see this visual multiple times, and it will likely become part of your daily life as you use it to find your compass and chart your course.

Throughout this book, you will find ideas and resources to help you to dig deeper into each of these quadrants. We will highlight educators who *are achieving this unicorn called "balance" or just getting it done,* and we encourage you to connect with others and to share what you are learning about living a more balanced life via Twitter at #BalanceLAP.

We also included additional resources. *Treasures from the Deep* are examples from people in the field learning and growing while finding balance in the journey. *Navigating the Course* are the ways we are meeting the challenges in each of the quadrants. *Cannonballs to Avoid* are the things that might sidetrack or stall you out from this work. *Set Sail* gives you guided questions to consider in this work, and how it can be implemented in your life.

The three of us do not have all the answers, nor do we live perfectly balanced lives. Honestly, most days we are a glorified "hot mess" in one quadrant or another. But we each have a passion to equip ourselves so we can accomplish our tasks and grow through our experiences every day.

SECTION ONE
PIRATE BALANCE

We cannot do it all, have
it all, or master it all.
That is simply not a thing.

—Jen Hatmaker

Do you ever feel like you want to do it all—but never feel like you are enough? If so, you certainly not alone. High achievers constantly hear internal reminders that push us to do more:

- I didn't work out enough
- I haven't helped my child study enough
- I didn't do enough lesson planning this week
- I didn't spend enough time with my spouse

It goes on and on and on. Social media doesn't help this dilemma. Every second you can see a new post, tweet, or video of incredibly awesome things others are doing, and immediately we have self-talk that diminishes our value and makes us feel as though we don't measure up or we are not enough. #BalanceLAP is an opportunity to stop beating ourselves up, focus on what we *can* do, and spend time developing ourselves in the different quadrants of balance.

We have had countless conversations with each other as well as educators we work with or are connected to, and we've found many incredible educators in the same sinking ship. Because we are so passionate about our professions and care deeply about our fellow educators, we wanted to create a resource to help others.

None of us is safe from imbalance. Because of this, we believe our message will resonate with you, but we also deeply hope we can build a community so you don't feel you are alone. More specifically, we intend to provide insights to free you from the limitations you put on yourself and help stem burnout in our profession.

The PIRATE Educator

To frame and guide this conversation, we use the PIRATE acronym to convey the sense of urgency we need to have about regaining balance, letting go of what we can't control, and freeing up space to learn and grow.

Passion: Balanced educators are passionate about purpose! Many educators start with overflowing amounts of passion, and their devotion is apparent. Passionate educators continue to pursue aspirations in all areas of life. Just because you grow up doesn't mean you outgrow creating new goals. Want to run a marathon? Write a book? Go back to school? Develop leadership skills? Learn to cook? Finding your passion can be the first step toward regaining purpose and happiness.

Immersion: Balanced educators immerse themselves in what they are engaged in, in all areas of their lives. Their life mantra is "Whatever you do, do it well." Balanced educators jump into an experience with both feet and are not distracted by the variety of demands because they are committed and intentional in their focus, thoughts, and words.

Rapport: Balanced educators know building and sustaining relationships are among the most important priorities! Because education is a people-driven field, relationships are paramount at work. But they are also crucial at home. Balanced educators understand their devotion to relationships in the various areas of life may collide at times, and they need to make choices about priority. Their choices, however, are always made with a caring heart and respect, which helps to mitigate guilt. If your relationships are built on enduring foundations, they will thrive through the balancing of different seasons requiring more or less of your time.

Ask and **A**nalyze: Balanced educators are reflective and aware of the amount of energy they place in the various spaces of their lives. They also know where they need to devote more or less energy. Reflection is critical to see details and execute a goal with precision and accuracy. Asking the right questions and analyzing truthful responses assist you to get on track when you fall off course. This process also helps you dig in deeper to focus and get real with yourself about what needs to change when you are off balance.

Transformation: Balanced educators are wise, courageous, and strong enough to take action to become the best versions of themselves. Transforming is a critical and cyclical phase. Seeking balance means you are constantly recalibrating. If you do this regularly, the transformation process is not so intense. But if you allow yourself to get too far out of balance, the process can be forced upon you by life changes stemming from your lack of healthy balance. Creating boundaries, setting goals, and becoming accountable for these changes is an evolving process—one necessary for the remainder of your days.

Enthusiasm: Balanced educators emanate enthusiasm for life because their energy is generated from the core. Their presence and energy in all aspects of life are important for those around them, and their enthusiasm is contagious and often reciprocated. Positive psychology and life experience prove this, and balanced educators can do all-important work with a joyful heart. Learning to live, lead, and teach with excitement and energy is critical not only to sustain the work, but to thrive through the rough spots.

Balance Is a Myth

No matter what compelled you to read this book, we're betting you have your own personal struggle and story about why you are seeking balance. Unfortunately, we have some bad news. The truth is, balance is a myth. There is no balance between work and home.

But wait, don't stop reading! Yes, it is impossible to find balance where professional and personal obligations are perfectly aligned, life runs smoothly every moment of the day, and you have a calm sense of well-being. Finding this type of balance would be like discovering a flying unicorn! So if someone tells you they found it, they're either lying—or in denial. And if you do happen to catch a glimpse of the "flying unicorn," we guarantee you will only see it briefly. The truth is, we go through ebbs and flows between feelings of sacrifice and renewal.

The key to thriving through the elusiveness of balance is to incessantly seek it, recalibrate often, intentionally focus on all aspects of your full life, and never give up! You are too important in the lives of students, staff, community, your network, and your family to walk off the education plank for good. Stick with us through this book. You will find treasure to sustain your course, we promise.

PASSION

Successful people do daily what
unsuccessful people do occasionally.
—John Maxwell

I don't have to chase extraordinary moments to
find happiness—it's right in front of me if I'm
paying attention and practicing gratitude.
—Brené Brown

Passion is the difference between
having a job or having a career.
—Unknown

*Y*ou wake up in the morning thinking about your students, and you go to bed the same way. Throughout the day your thoughts are filled with what to do next, what went well, and what you need to improve. Even outside of the school day you can't turn it off, dinnertime, family time, even on your evening walk or morning run, you just can't stop. Until one day, you literally wake up. You realize you are missing the joy of the moments because you are so caught up in what is coming up next, what needs to be planned or accomplished. You are exhausted, you are unhappy, and you might be burning out.

Many educators are at risk of Sacrifice Syndrome, a concept written about in the book *The Resonant Leader*. If you're reading this book, you're probably at risk. Sometimes it can be hard to tell when you are slipping into this syndrome because you often get there by passion. For example, educators are passionate about their work; they want to go the extra mile to do their best for kids. They often volunteer for extra commitments or have a hard time saying "no" when asked to take on an extra task or role, and find joy in attempting to overcome obstacles in the way of helping students learn and grow. Letting passion for your work take over your life is easy and can happen before you realize you are sacrificing your personal and family life.

While there is no secret to achieving true balance, there are ways to create healthy boundaries between home and work so you can feel a sense of renewal each morning, ready to give one hundred percent to your staff and students. Just as you are a passionate educator continuing to learn and grow in your craft, you must also learn ways to be more efficient with your time management and organization. This will equip you to almost effortlessly handle the "stuff" piling up on you, allowing you to spend your time and mental energy on truly important work.

Jessica. Can you have too much of a good thing? I did. During the past school year, I was given a ton of blessings in my professional life that sparked great passions! I was training for a marathon with my dear friend Adam Welcome, I was the Minnesota Distinguished Principal traveling to Washington D.C., and I was speaking across Minnesota. Oh, and I was writing two books at the same time. During the season I was as balanced as I could be, and while I was grateful for every single opportunity and blessing, I quickly recognized that my passions were overtaking all other quadrants. With a great deal of reflection, and some very brutal and honest conversations with my spouse, my dear friends, and coworkers, I made a very difficult decision and took a different course in my career. I applied, interviewed for, and was offered the middle school principal position, the school where my oldest son was attending and where my younger son would be in a few years. Stepping back and recalibrating what my priorities were was hard, but five years from now, I won't regret the choice I made today. ■

So many aspects of this role are completely out of your control and can cause a great deal of stress (as we discuss more in Section Three). The one thing you *can* control is creating time for activities you know are beneficial to your personal sense of calm and balance—and necessary to offset the cannonballs coming your way. Let's be clear here. We are not talking about turning your educational role into a "clock in and out" job where you take the easy way out and are not good for kids. That's not you. You went into education with passion and purpose, and we know you want to continue to grow and have impact every day. But you also need to learn ways to balance your professional and personal life so you give your best to your students and staff each day and set a great example for them as well.

Ensuring you are monitoring and remembering the reason for your purpose and revisiting your "why" are incredibly important because factors often threaten to sink you slowly.

Passion from Positivity

Sarah. As a high-school administrator, I sometimes hear from teachers, "I wouldn't want your job," or, "I couldn't do what you do." Usually their comments are prompted by a recent disciplinary issue, a tough decision, or amidst dissent among staff. My response is always the same and always genuine: "There is nothing I would rather do than be here for you and the students." ■

Of course, sometimes it is harder to remain positive through every challenge without doubt in our hearts. You know the days—the ones with multiple fires to put out, looming deadlines, perception-survey results making you feel inadequate, demands from supervisors, complaints from students, angry parent messages, and to top it off, the "air" you chewed on for breakfast, lunch, and dinner didn't quite satisfy or fortify you! On these days especially, it is critical to find your joy. Otherwise, comments like the ones from Sarah's teachers can seep in and make you question yourself for staying in your role.

Joy isn't found in outside forces. The truth is you cannot depend on people or things to bring you joy or happiness. If you fall into the trap of expecting they can, you will forever be disappointed. Your spouse will never measure up, your children will disappoint, and your friends and family will often fail to feed your happiness quota. Seeking joy from validation or praise is a losing battle—your phone and email will not often fill up with effusive praise for the daily miracles you perform. You need to discover your personal joys, develop diverse habits to consistently boost endorphin levels, and keep moving passionately through each day, week, term, year, and into the next cycle. This is how you thrive for many years to come.

Positive psychology teaches our vibes are contagious. Unfortunately, this is true for positive *or* negative vibes, and an ugly cycle can form in education if the culture isn't healthy enough to combat negativity.

Sarah. I consider myself one of the lucky ones in education. Not only have I stuck with this career, but I have thrived and continue to love it each day. This is nothing short of a minor miracle, given how my career started. I taught my first two years without my own classroom, utilizing a cart to transport my materials. My coursework responsibility included grades six through twelve in a small school where I also taught instructional television *and* coordinated all in-service training sessions *and* led a team of teachers to implement the Six Traits of Writing throughout our district in kindergarten through twelfth grade. All the while, one of my colleagues frequently reminded me my position was grant funded, and I would not have a job the next year. Complaining from burned-out staff about administration was constant. And according to some colleagues, the students would never leave town; they would work in the mill as their families had for decades. I distinctly remember making a conscientious decision to find my joy and focus my attention on the students.

Entering my second year as an educator, I had never read a book on positive psychology nor heard the term "blog," and PLNs or Twitter didn't exist yet. I was a relatively unconnected educator and the only English teacher in the high school of ninety students (and remained so for most of my years in the classroom). Because I knew I wouldn't survive in education if my life was entrenched in negativity, my mantra in my second year was to be an *intentional* "Positive Polly"—not a "Negative Nelly." (Yes, I was an English teacher steeped in alliteration at the time!)

A new principal arrived at this time, and the remaining years in this beautiful school were some of the best of my career. I sang to my students on their birthdays, lovingly gave them nicknames, showed videos of babies laughing to release my students' endorphins before major paper-writing sessions, planned and performed in talent shows for students, smiled every day, and made sure to laugh my signature loud laugh daily. Being intentionally positive fortified me and created a ripple that affected those around me. Because I sought my joy intentionally and revisited my passionate purpose, this position also remains a highlighted chapter in a career with, hopefully, many chapters left. ■

We want to hand Sarah's gems to the educators in our buildings and those of you reading this book. Positivity produces energy and endorphins in the brain. You must not forget to intentionally choose to be positive to keep yourselves fresh, productive for your students, and full of passion.

Treasures from the Deep:
A Practitioner's Passion

Tiawana Giles, MEd, @TiawanaG,
assistant principal, Richmond, Virginia

Being a mom, daughter, wife, grandparent, and school administrator can present many challenges. But with those challenges come opportunities to prioritize the passion I have for life and how I choose to lead it. I set boundaries, reflect daily, connect with my PLN on Twitter—all through my Google calendar. Living a life with passion has contributed to my success at work and my happiness at home in my personal life. Having passion in all I do also requires that I be patient and intentional with my time and say "no" to things inconsistent with my mantra, mission, and passions.

I am passionate about:

- Connecting with my PLN via Twitter.
- Working with kids. I became a teacher because I believe kids are our future, and I want to be a part of molding the next generation. My role has evolved, and I now help kids find their own passions.
- Coaching educators. I work closely with teachers at every level in my building to help them be successful.
- Engaging with the community. I believe it is essential to support our families and help them navigate through the educational process.

- Providing a safe learning environment. I work closely with our students to let them know I love them. I have high expectations of them; I will always follow up and follow through.
- Balancing work, school, and home. I run about three miles a week and read leadership books when I wake up and before going to bed. These things help me keep a life-work balance.
- Helping my family. I have a supportive husband, two daughters, and one granddaughter. My husband and I still have date nights, and I support my daughters in every way possible.

My Best Advice on Balance
- Build a network of peers you can work with, bounce ideas off, and be accountable to.
- Schedule breaks and boundaries to take care of yourself.
- Take time to be a parent, grandparent, spouse, friend, and colleague. Don't ever forget who you are and what you are meant to be.
- Learn to take criticism and feedback and develop a thick skin. Own your weaknesses and look for ways to improve.

Set Sail

- Take a minute to revisit your purpose. What propelled you into education? Why did you choose this profession?

- What about your profession fuels your passion?

- On a scale of "one to burnout," where are you currently? If your passion flames are high, how can you keep them stoked? If they are nearly extinguished, keep reading.

Tweet it out with #BalanceLAP.

Immersion

Whatever you do, do it well.
—Walt Disney

H ave you ever gotten so engaged in a movie, book, or conversation you completely lost track of time? Jumping into your life with both feet—and no life jacket—can be incredibly exhilarating. But far too often, you can be distracted by the noise of your role: upcoming meetings, observations to complete, upset parents or stakeholders, approaching deadlines—the list goes on and on. The noise, if not controlled, can overwhelm the calm and quiet you need to be fully present in what you do.

Immersion into your life requires an intentional commitment to be present, focused, and intentional with your thoughts, words, and actions. Setting aside time, putting your phone away, and shutting your office door are environmental supports to help decrease your mental distractions. But until you truly understand the value of connecting fully with others and engaging in life one hundred percent, you won't have buy-in.

Think about trying to have a conversation with someone when they are on their phone. Do you think they are really hearing you? Do you feel heard? Now turn the table. Do you multitask when a student or staff member talks you? At staff meetings, are you listening to the current conversation or thinking about what is next on your schedule? While sticking to your plan for your day is important, you need to make sure you are engaged in your current calendar item instead of focusing on what just happened or what is coming next.

As teachers, principals, and parents, we can usually tell if someone really did their homework or just rushed through to get it done. The same is true in life. If something is worth doing—do it well. Setting aside time and immersing yourself in a project, paper, or lesson—with focus and a specific target in mind—can give you clarity for the quality of work and time needed to complete it. Be careful your work isn't clouded by the newest Facebook ad or pin on Pinterest, but filled with a clearinghouse of research of what works and the rationale behind the why. Immersing yourself in your life *is* your life.

We value being connected on social media, and learning and growing from our PLN. However, being connected is a double-edged sword. The obvious risk is being connected at the expense of those around you in real life. But it is also exceptionally easy to become overwhelmed by the myriad of ideas being shared. Balancing your excitement about new ideas to try with feelings of envy of those sharing or inadequacy for not doing more can be hard. Do *not* become so immersed in social media you take on too much and overwhelm yourself, or you feel like you're not doing enough.

One of our favorite authors, Brené Brown, describes social media so well in *Braving the Wilderness*: "I've come to the conclusion that the way we engage with social media is like fire—you can use [it] to keep yourself warm and nourished, or you can burn down the barn. It all depends on your intentions, expectations, and reality-checking skills."

Wow. Just wow. How are you engaging with social media? Are you using these tools to grow personally and professionally, or are you allowing them, unintentionally, to become negative voices in your life? Comparison is a thief of joy in all facets of your life, and comparing yourself to anyone on the Internet is sure cause for doubt and feelings of failure. You are the captain of your ship. You are navigating the course, so stop looking around at everyone else. Focus on where you want to go, and get after it!

"Life Moves Pretty Fast"

Life moves pretty fast. If you don't stop and look around once in a while, you might miss it.
—Ferris Bueller, *Ferris Bueller's Day Off*

Writing this book has reminded us how quickly time passes and if we don't fully invest in the moments, they will vanish. Coordinating a writing retreat with three very different schedules landed us on a weekend in the middle of December. While each of us missed activities at home, emails we could have answered, or paperwork we could have finished before Monday, we dedicated forty-eight hours to a passion project—one tapping into all four quadrants of balance. Our commitment meant we were totally immersed in the project during those hours and not distracted by our other responsibilities. You've likely had those moments of guilt—doing something you need or want to do—but worrying about what you are missing while doing it.

By letting go of the guilt, you open yourself up to be fully immersed in the moments quickly going by.

Jessica. When I look at young families, I often feel great regret because, for the first few years of my oldest son's life, I didn't have this mindset of immersion or enjoying just *being*. I filled every minute of every day with *something*. Many times the minutes overlapped, leaving me with fatigue, frustration, and a lack of "fully present" in any of my interactions. Understandably, we all make sacrifices for what we believe is the greater good, but if our priorities are out of line, we might be losing out on the people and experiences most important down the road. I am in the true "middle place" in my life: I can see as far forward as I can backwards, and I have formed many memories and relationships in my "fortyish" years of life. When I have the opportunity to attend a memorial service of a friend, coworker, or family member, I never think I spent *too much* time with the person when she was living. I always remember the time we spent together and wish for *more* time. ■

Do your best to be fully present and immerse yourself in your life. You may end up saying "no" to some things or not getting something you thought you wanted. But you will have strong memories and firm relationships with those who truly matter to you. In the end, this is what matters most.

Treasures from the Deep: Focusing on Being Present

Josh Lichty, fifth-grade teacher, Wisconsin

I have great memories of playing Trivial Pursuit as a kid. The goal was to work around the board (picture a wagon wheel with spokes connecting it to a middle core), answering questions from six different categories to get to the six wedge spaces, each a different color. If I missed the "pie-earning question" for one color, sometimes I would start to move around the circle toward a different-colored wedge, forgetting about the color I missed until later on.

The idea of immersion and creating deep, mental involvement with an activity makes me rethink the way the Trivial Pursuit board was created. I would eliminate the outer ring. Instead, the path to each wedge space would only go through the center core. This would mean once I went down the path and reached the wedge space, my focus would only be on correctly answering the "pie-earning question." Then I would return to the center core before moving on to the next category.

How does this relate to immersion of balanced educators? Think about everything on our plates as our pie pieces. My pieces might be excelling as a father to my eight-year-old daughter, being the best fifth-grade teacher, coaching my football team to an undefeated season, growing in my faith, striving for better health and fitness, and growing in my relationships with friends and family. Each activity deserves my full focus—of time, attention, and energy. If I worry about one area while trying to focus on another, I am not being the best in the moment in either area. For example, I've tried to read continuing education books while on the exercise bike. I do not get a good workout, nor do I retain the information. This also goes with raising my daughter. If I work on correcting papers when I'm with her, she's not getting what she deserves. I'm a better dad when I give her all of me, and work on correcting papers we are apart.

A game board with no outer ring provides two benefits in our actual lives. First, once we are in our desired activity, there are no distractions. Focus solely on the current "game piece" until you have accomplished your task. Secondly, *always* go back to your core before you go to the next area of your life. Get back to who you are—your beliefs and values—before moving on. Take a breath, recenter, refocus, and get excited about where you are going next. This is how you earn your "pie pieces." This is how to be a winner!

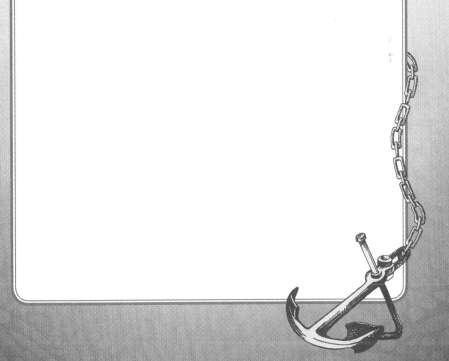

Set Sail

- Where in your life are you immersed at this time? Are you satisfied with the level of intentional energy you are giving in this space?

- When you are immersed in a project or focused on a task, do you feel joyful? If so, how can you bring that to other spaces? If not, reflect about why this is so.

Tweet it out with #BalanceLAP.

RAPPORT

Relationships, relationships, relationships.
—Jimmy Casas

Invisible threads are the strongest ties.
—Friedrich Nietzsche

In any context, the outcome of your interactions with others has a direct correlation with the relationships you have—or haven't—built with them. Developing rapport with others can be an incredibly powerful way to learn from them and find common ground moving forward. Rapport does more than give you what you want from a conversation with someone. It can lead to a deeper understanding of another person's perspective, and in turn might change your own mind. Rapport is especially important as you chart your course toward balance. In a world where balance doesn't come naturally, you're going to have to ask others for help.

Rapport begins with being vulnerable and honest, opening doors for conversations, assistance, and collaboration. As educators, you need to model for your students that you are actually lifelong learners, you don't hold all the knowledge to impart to them (*gasp!*), and you have as much to learn as you have to teach. Admitting you don't know everything allows your students—or your staff if you're a leader in education—to see you as "normal." *This also gives you grace to quit trying to climb up on the pedestal you think everyone expects to see you on.*

Jessica. As I pursue growth in this area, I find people who naturally build rapport, and I spend time studying them to see how they position their body towards the person they are talking to, how they mirror specific points of the conversation, or use the other person's name so naturally in the conversation. Even in the grocery store, my "rapport" mentors always have time for a question or a conversation; they never appear to be rushed, hurried, or frazzled. Learning from them, I have sticky notes in my office where I can "park" a thought I have while I'm engaged in a conversation with another person. This allows me to stay mentally focused on what the other person is saying without losing the thought. At home, if one of my boys starts talking to me while I am doing something else, I ask him to "hold his thought" until I finish and turn to face him and listen, distraction free.

Rapport is also built by our intentions during a conversation or being mentally prepared to hold a conversation.

I used to enter conversations with a "fixer" mentality, always feeling the other person wanted me to fix what he was talking about. I am learning sometimes people just want me to listen. I've learned the importance of "checking myself" before a conversation. If I just broke up a fight at school or received difficult personal news, quickly shifting gears to hold a conversation with someone is a struggle for me. Whenever possible, I take three to five minutes to recalibrate before the next appointment on my calendar. I might walk around the school, help a student tie her shoe, or lock myself in the staff bathroom (Don't judge until you try it!). The break allows me to briefly reflect on what just happened, make any mental notes of what I need to do later, and gain focus for my next task. ■

Building Rapport Capital

You will walk away with a new frame of mind and a deeper relationship with the other person if you enter and exit every conversation with another person asking, "How will I grow or become better from this interaction?"

Educators have a myriad of opportunities every day to build rapport through interactions with others. While you have a choice about where to spend your energy, it is important to consider it only takes a thirty-second conversation to help someone feel noticed, cared for, and important. When you take time to look a person in the eye, ask how you can help, or simply listen to his thoughts, you engage in important work. Those interactions build a relationship bank account, gaining interest. If you choose in any given moment to ignore another person or rush past her in the hallway without at least a smile, you miss an opportunity to build rapport capital.

Sarah. I am always making myself vulnerable: I sing to students, ask them what their plans are for the weekend, listen to their complaints, and never miss an opportunity to tell them they matter. I do this to build rapport and strengthen my relationship with them. Some of the students who need me the most will likely not initiate a conversation about what is happening in their life if I don't open up to nurture that relationship first. They need me to know their story and see their whole picture. When they make a mistake involving dire consequences, they need me to remember the details of their life possibly leading to this turning point. ■

Possessing emotional intelligence and the capacity to build and sustain rapport with their learning community is essential for educators. Sometimes this is as easy as a secret handshake with a student who has been struggling with peers. Other times it is as difficult as swallowing pride and admitting fault when you have not followed through with something or you are expelling a student. But at the heart of everything are the relationships you develop and maintain. Balanced educators must consider how to pour themselves out without emptying their own cup. This comes with the reciprocal benefits of authentic, genuine rapport building.

Deep Threads and Strong Tethers

What is most meaningful in any area of our lives are the deep threads and strong tethers we build in our relationships with people we encounter on our life journey. Consider those deep threads that we weave through the days and years with people in our personal and professional lives that develop into abiding and lasting relationships. These are the individuals with whom we create history through shared experience and meaningful interactions. In our personal lives, we most often think of close family, intimate friends, and our longest lasting relationships. We know about the details of these people's lives, and they share some of our monumental life experiences. They walk with us through the staid and steady days, carry us during struggle, and dance along to the shared tune in the glory times of our lives. Like any relationship, the deep threads take time and work with intentional focus and honor given to those partnerships.

In our positional and professional lives, we create deep threads with people through shared experiences that connect us in more profound ways than the occasional team meeting or interaction. In these spaces, deep threads are woven through daily interactions, intentional acts of caring, and vulnerable leaps of faith. We can build these connections with our students, colleagues, school families, and community partners and the connections can be just as strong as those in our personal lives over time. We work hard at this in our professional and positional lives because these relationships are not always natural. They may manifest out of conflict or chaos, develop from common interest or divergent opinions, or they may emerge out of our capacity to show unassuming kindness in people's hours of deepest need. I (Sarah) have been known to engage in bold ways with students when there is a concerning behavior. Recently, my district administrator trusted me enough to respond to a 6:30 a.m. text requesting to take a student out for breakfast to build a relationship. This student had been struggling with peer groups, depression, and frankly displayed behaviors that many cast as a potential threat. That morning for breakfast took some of our time, but it built a relationship with a student who needed to be heard and a parent who desired for a child to be seen. *Deepen the threads. Take the time to build those relationships.*

Strong tethers are a product of both of those intentionally built deep threads and an innate ability to connect with another human being. Our own professional learning network as coauthors is a perfect demonstration of this as we have morphed into a personal *lean-in* network from the strong tethers we have developed over time.

Balancing like a pirate means that we take time to intentionally build deep threads and strong tethers with those around us to keep ourselves in balance.

JJ Having been a principal in my school for ten years, I have had the privilege of building long-standing relationships with families over the years. Being in a pre-K through twelfth-grade building, it is not unusual for a middle- or high-school student to seek me out in the elementary wing about something happening in their life, positive or negative. While some students' behaviors have consumed much of my time, I look at what we see happening in school. Instead of asking, "What is wrong with you?" I ask, "What has happened to you?" Almost always, when students are acting out in school, it is a response to what is happening in their life outside of school.

I had built a strong connection with "Sabrina" and her family, having worked with them over seven years. Sabrina had some behavior issues in school, but for years had done fine in class, with occasional breaks in my office, where she would draw, use a meditation app, and regularly water my plant (an official job I gave her that she took pride in). One day, her behaviors became so severe, with harm to self and others, that it required a long and taxing physical restraint with myself and other staff members. It felt like it went on forever, because her parents were unresponsive to the situation. We were frightened for her; we were becoming exhausted and unsure of what to do. At one point, her body calmed and she turned to me, latched on with a hug, and just sobbed. Trained by her parents to not tell anyone what happens at home, she still didn't tell what was bothering her, but she did finally disclose that home is not good and she's just afraid.

Later, when mom finally picked her up, the relationship with the family became more evident when Sabrina asked her mom if she could just go with me that night, because she knew I was going to watch a sporting event in another town. Having been completely exhausted from my day with her, my immediate reaction was that I wanted a break from this child. However, I realized what a strong tether I had created with Sabrina that she wanted to spend more time with me after such an event. Even more telling about the deep threads built with this family was when her mother turned to me and said, "I think it would be safer if she went with you tonight." ∎

Treasures from the Deep: Witnessing the Power of Relationships

Anonymous

I serve as the hearing officer in student discipline situations in our district office. My goal in these meetings is to allow the building administrators, parents, and students to share their perspectives on incidents so I can gather information for possible disciplinary action. Having studied the board policies, student handbooks, state rules and processes, I take pride in the processes I had created to conduct an efficient, nonconfrontational meeting.

During one meeting, I was beginning to make closing comments when the principal asked for permission to speak. Although my normal process didn't allow for this, the participants were amicable so I agreed. The principal prefaced his next words with an apology to the parents, and proceeded to tell them their child was lying.

I was mortified, and I started to get angry. *Why would he do this?* Looking for a professional way to end the meeting before it got worse, I turned to the principal to make eye contact, but he continued to talk with the parents and student.

With gentleness in his voice, he told them he cared for their child and was scared that her risky behaviors could lead to more, severe harm in the future. He told the parents he wouldn't be doing his job if he didn't intervene and bring out the real needs for her safety and well-being.

He talked to the student, retelling stories of her from past years which seemed to describe a different student, and then pointed out the changes he had seen in her during the past few months. He told them he wanted the best for her and wanted to see her graduate. At that point, he turned to me and told me of a conversation he had with the student last year about her dream job and about his work with her since then to guide her to make it a reality. After he finished speaking, the student—and her parents—began to cry. Her parents finally spoke up, asking for help. They agreed their daughter was engaging in risky behaviors, but they didn't know how to address it. During the meeting, the parents' tactic had changed from backing their daughter to asking for help with her. The principal and I identified resources we could provide at school and connections we could make with local organizations to support her and her family at home. We defined actions not only to ensure she could graduate on time, but to address her social-emotional needs as well.

After the family left, I debriefed with the principal, and he apologized for interrupting the meeting. Amazed at what had just happened, I thanked him for not only speaking up, but for building a positive rapport with his students and families. His rapport allowed for real help to happen. Our conversation couldn't have taken place if the principal had not cultivated a relationship with the student prior to the meeting. Because of his rapport, he knew the right thing to truly help her and was able to address this hard issue. Building positive rapport with students is vital for real conversations and transformational leadership to take place.

Set Sail

- Which relationships in your life are characterized by deep threads and strong tethers? How have you deepened and maintained those connections?

- Which relationships in your life need a jolt of energy? How can you be intentional in your approach to developing stronger connections?

- In what ways have you worked to build rapport daily with your learning community? What steps have others taken that you might consider adding to your routine?

- What about your profession fuels your passion?

Tweet it out with #BalanceLAP.

ASK AND ANALYZE

The more reflective you are, the more effective you are.
—Pete Hall and Alisa Simeral

Educators' days are fast paced. From the moment their alarms go off, until their brains finally shut off and allow them to sleep, they feel like they are *sprinting* in a marathon. You know the feeling! However, you also know you will never make it to the end of the course if you are sprinting. You must pace yourself—slow down—hydrate—refuel. You are constantly moving from one thing to the next, with very little time for a bathroom break or to eat lunch sitting down—let alone time to pause and reflect on what's working and what's not.

But you must pause—and reflect.

Evidence supports time for reflection to help the learning process. It is even referred to as the "stickiest glue for the brain." In fact, John Dewey writes, "We do not learn from experience...we learn from reflecting on experience." Good teachers provide time for students to reflect on learning goals, but do they create time to reflect personally? Do you ask and analyze to maintain the balance you need to be your best?

If you pay attention to yourself, you can tell when you are off balance.

Sarah. When I'm off balance, I'm exhausted to the point I cannot do anything after my girls go to bed. In fact, I may even fall asleep myself while putting one of them to bed. If I am drinking more coffee than normal or eating junk food as my main source of nutrition, my balance is off. At these times, I realize I have not talked to my parents or siblings in weeks, and I generally feel less hopeful and struggle seeing the joy in the days. ■

Maybe your clues include going to work earlier and getting home later each day, or finding you can never relax and enjoy something for personal pleasure unless you've had a glass of wine at night to shut your brain off. Well-known fitness trainer Jillian Michaels shared on social media, "We take care of our phones better than our bodies. We know when our battery is depleted." What a powerful statement! If you know when your phone battery needs to be recharged, then you really should know when you need to refuel yourself. What if you took just as much care of yourself as you do your phone?

You are likely familiar with Stephen Covey's story about the "big rocks." When given the task of filling a jar with sand, gravel, and rocks, the only way to complete the task is to put the big rocks in first, then the gravel, and finally the sand to fill the small crevices. If you fill your day with "sand"—tedious tasks with little impact or value—you will not have time for the most important work. You must first put in the big rocks—the most impactful tasks on your calendar.

This story is a great reminder of the importance of routinely reflecting on the quadrants in your life. What are your "big rocks" in each area? What work or focus in each area is the most important for you? Which of the quadrants is more important for you at this point in time? As we've said, you will never achieve true balance; you can't expect to have twenty-five percent in each area. Life just does not work out mathematically. There will be times when one quadrant takes more time and mental energy than the others.

JJ. My life turned upside down when my son had a life-threatening baseball injury during a summer when I was scheduled for several professional-development conferences. His injury landed him in the hospital for several weeks while he had six surgeries to repair his ruptured nasal arteries and I rarely left his side even to use the bathroom. Obviously, my focus turned to taking care of him, and the other quadrants of my life were all put on hold.

Hopefully life won't always throw such curveballs (though my son is quick to correct me, his accident was from a fly ball!), but a new job will definitely cause your positional and professional quadrant to require more time and focus. A personal health diagnosis may increase the time and focus your personal quadrant needs as you implement new exercise or nutrition habits into your life. However, it is still important to pay some attention to your other quadrants during these "off-balance" times so they aren't neglected and lead to burnout.

Having a personal mission statement, affirmation, or mantra for each quadrant can help give you focus.

I have written personal affirmations for each quadrant of my life and read them each morning to set my focus. For example, for my personal quadrant, my affirmation is: *I am a devoted wife and mother. My goals/work should be good modeling for my children, but should not get in the way of being present to enjoy my time with them to help them grow into the best people they can be. I want to make sure that I connect with each of them every evening.* ■

What? So What? What Now?

The "What? So What? What Now?" model is a great reflection model to use with students or teachers and also seems fitting for asking and analyzing. Take some time right now to reflect on your current status, using the quadrants and these questions to reflect:

- What is currently filling each of the quadrants in your life? (Go ahead and just list everything that comes to mind for you, including all of the "gravel" and "sand.")
- Using a different color pen or a new blank quadrant, what are your priorities in each quadrant? (Whether they are currently being followed or not.)
- With yet another color (or another blank quadrant), what activities would be ideal for you to live out your priorities in each quadrant of your life?
- What needs to change in your day-to-day life to prioritize these goals? What small tweaks can you make so these big rocks go into your daily jar first?
- Take your priorities one step further and write out a positive affirmation for each. A positive affirmation is a short, positive statement intended to help you focus on your goals, getting rid of your negative, self-deprecating beliefs. When you recite your positive affirmations each morning to start your day with intention, it is like you are reprogramming your brain with positivity to focus on your priorities and goals. All you need to do is take your priority, goal, or intention you want to instill in your mindset and turn it into a positive statement for yourself. Here are some examples:
  - Every day, in every way, I'm getting better and better.
  - I eat well, exercise regularly, and get plenty of rest to enjoy good health.

- I accept what I cannot change.
- I practice patience, understanding, and compassion with others as well as myself.

As you continue reading, refer back to your quadrants and personal goals to help you find your compass and chart your course. Start each day out reciting your affirmations to yourself. Yes, this will feel weird at first, but we promise it is worth it. By the "law of attraction," you will attract into your life whatever you focus on. When you start out your day with positivity and intentionality, you will automatically attract more good and positive things into your life.

Treasures from the Deep: Awareness and Adjustment

Melinda Miller, @mmiller7571,
elementary principal, Springfield, Missouri

When I met Jessica Johnson on Twitter nine years ago, we joked about principals living on "isolation island." Since then, I have met hundreds of professional friends who share my passions, and I have connections and collaboration at my fingertips—literally. Social media changed my life.

But then I fell out of balance. My online relationships took the place of real-life relationships. Because I was too busy with the daily issues of being principal, I couldn't collaborate with my online colleagues during the day. So I started to connect with them on evenings and weekends, and my family started to take a backseat.

Being a principal is a calling for me. However, I am also called to be a wife, mom, daughter, etc. Career and family do not have to be at odds when trying to find balance; however, there is not a magical life-balance scale. I can't put eight hours on the "work" side of the scale and eight hours on the "family" side and—boom!—I have balance. I had to find what worked for me. Participating in Twitter chats for two hours a night, five days a week wasn't working, but scheduling one or two a week is manageable. Listening to Voxer for an hour in the morning and another hour in the evening didn't work for my family and me, but listening on the weekend or one night during a workout is manageable.

I don't beat myself up about balance anymore. Also, I no longer compartmentalize the different areas of my life—my family blends in with my work, and my work blends in with my family. For example, this week I may not bring work home at all; next week, I might have to work from home two nights. This weekend I can to listen to all my Voxer groups; next weekend I'll probably have to declare "Voxer bankruptcy" and delete them all. Tonight is pizza and movie night with my girls; tomorrow night they may be eating cereal while watching TV because I have deadlines to meet.

After twenty-five years in education, my journey to find balance is still evolving. I just have to continuously ask myself what is working, what is not, and be responsive to all areas of my life. Balance doesn't have to be one *or* another. I can have it all–just not all the time.

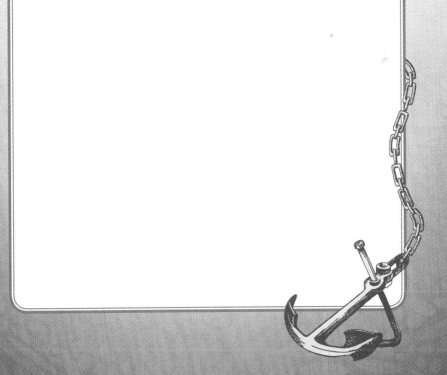

Set Sail

What are your "tells" for being off balance? Reflect on a time when you felt unsatisfied with one or each of your balance quadrants (*personal, professional, positional, passions*) and answer the following questions:

- Why were you dissatisfied?

- Did you receive any feedback from others helping you identify you were "off track"?

- What signs indicated things weren't cohesive?

- How can you avoid this state in the future?

- Which quadrant do you feel needs the most work at this time?

- Where are you thriving?

- Start your new habit of reviewing your positive affirmations each morning. See how you feel after one week of this and review how it has changed you.

Tweet it out with #BalanceLAP.

TRANSFORMATION

We do not need magic to transform
our world. We carry all the power we
need inside ourselves already.
—J.K. Rowling

The most authentic thing about us
is our capacity to create, to overcome,
to endure, to transform, to love, and
to be greater than our suffering.
—Ben Okri

It's only after you've stepped outside
your comfort zone that you begin to
change, grow, and transform.
—Roy T. Bennett

Transformation takes acknowledging a need to change, courage to venture into the process, patience through the pruning, and commitment to become a more refined version of yourself. People are constantly in the process of transforming, and those who embrace becoming their best selves are the ones who inspire others. When you transform into a more balanced educator, everyone wins. While this transformation can be gradual—even painful—the results are worth so much because you will be full enough to pour out in ways that become reciprocally beneficial in all aspects of your life.

Be a Scrooge!

Ebenezer Scrooge is a quintessential example of transformation. (Personally, I [Sarah] love the Donald Duck version because my dad produced a stellar impersonation!) When Scrooge is introduced in *A Christmas Carol*, he is unbalanced—focusing his entire energy on his positional life. Throughout the story, though, Dickens reveals Scrooge had once been a balanced man, focused on building himself positionally, while also planning to marry a young woman he loved and who shared his life goals. Sadly, over time, Scrooge lost focus. His lack of balance created a fissure in his relationship, and the span of years produced an unbalanced miser only focused on work. In turn, he overworked his employees, pushed away family and friends, and ignored personal interests. As a result, he became passionless—even heartless.

However, through a series of unveiling visions, Scrooge transforms. He recognizes his lack of balance and realizes gaping chasms in his life must be filled. Literally overnight, he is a changed man—focusing on others and his personal life. Instead of working on Christmas Day, he spends it focusing on the people in his life.

People love this story of transformation. If Scrooge can turn around, anyone can! But you must understand change is cyclical. You never truly arrive in a space where you are "finished" transforming. You are not the same version of your eighteen-year-old self, nor are you the person you will be at ninety. Becoming a balanced educator is challenging because you have to navigate through a lot of changes!

For example, you may reach stasis within all aspects of your life only to find your balance thrown off by a promotion, the addition of a child, marriage, success with a passion, or professional growth through sharing with your PLN. Even these positive changes require you to make decisions about what you are gaining or sacrificing in the process of transformation. Unpredictable, and less positive, changes like the loss of a position, health, or family member can also force imbalance and require transformation we never expected.

Making Sacrifices

Transformation requires making choices and changes which can be painful. If you are an educator who is unbalanced in any area (this is all of us at times!), you are sacrificing something you love for another thing you love. Most educators choose their profession for the students, but the complex aspects required to impact students are never ending and can literally consume their lives.

Sarah. Before I had my own children, you could find me at school by 6:00 a.m., and I wouldn't leave until late in the evening. I spent evenings *and* weekends *and* lunch hours working. If I wasn't teaching, I was grading endless stacks of papers, attending events, fundraising for the groups I led, developing curriculum, leading student council activities—the list goes on. When my own children came into the picture, transformation had to occur. However, shifting focus away from my students and toward more balance was initially painful. I had to make painful decisions, pitting very deep and abiding passions against one another. In truth, I faced these same painful decisions again as my profession and position transformed. Transforming to a building administrator was intense and completely disrupted my balance during those years. In fact, my recent personal "unbalanced" experience is a direct result of not focusing intentionally on balance during my first year as an administrator. Habits I formed then had a dramatic impact on my family and threatened to crush us. I had to transform again. ■

You need to continuously and intentionally focus on your transformation, or your ship will list gradually off course through the changing seasons of your life. If we are not steering our vessels with intentional focus to change through the tides, shifts can occur that we may not intend. Just as a transformation can occur for the better, it can also sink us—the result of a slow leak from balance to being unbalanced.

So where are you right now? Does your life need a transformation? Maybe you need to focus on just one or two areas to transform into the balanced educator you want to be? Or maybe you need a complete overhaul because you've lost sight of several pieces of yourself. Regardless of where you are, get real with yourself. Acknowledge your need to change and courageously engage in the process of change. Be prepared for some pain in the pruning, knowing it is producing a better version of yourself. Can't wait to get started? You already have by reading this book! Keep reading to Section Four, where we share several actionable steps toward transformation into balance.

Treasures from the Deep

Akram Osman, @AkramMosman,
associate principal, Burnsville, MN

Finding your passion isn't just about careers and money. It's about finding your authentic self. The one you've buried beneath other people's needs.

—Kristin Hannah

I have experienced much growth as an educational leader in the past three years of my life, and that's because of a commitment I made to find my true authentic self. I have dedicated much of my time engaging in opportunities that gave me life and fed my soul with positivity! Those opportunities include spending quality time with family, especially my three young and beautiful nieces, connecting with a diverse group of educational leaders from all over the nation using social media, face-to-face connections, and phone conversations to help me lead and transform my school as a leader. I have also dedicated much time to running, which always makes me feel like I'm on top of this wonderful world!

I believe that I live in my passion and purpose daily and experience a great sense of fulfillment and gratitude. I have found balance in life by simply identifying things that feed my soul with positivity and keep me focused in my personal mission of impacting the lives of the people I'm lucky to serve. Being an educational leader is a demanding role, but with a clear mindset, a positive attitude, and opportunities that feed the soul, anything is possible!

Set Sail

- Are you currently undergoing a transformation? If so, is it intentional, or the result of a loss or addition in your life?

- Reflect on a time you made a major life change. Was this due to dissatisfaction, or a transformation into something better?

- What advice might you give someone who is undergoing a transformation and struggling with the change?

Tweet it out with #BalanceLAP.

ENTHUSIASM

Success is stumbling from failure to
failure with no loss of enthusiasm.
— Winston Churchill

Take action towards your dreams.
Walk your talk. Dance and sing to
your music. Embrace your blessings.
Make today worth remembering.
— Steve Maraboli

Maintaining enthusiasm for your varied roles is essential for deep and enduring impact. Being enthusiastic is easy when you are involved in something new and shiny—before the mundane takes over. For example, do you remember when you accepted your first job offer and rushed to prepare your classroom or office because you were so excited the space was *yours*? How about the first time you found out you were adding a new family member, or the first weeks of a new relationship? Was it hard to summon enthusiasm for the sheer experience of it? No! And no enthusiasm compares to what you pour out when you are gifted with your first professional position!

But after a while, trenching into monotony can reduce enthusiasm. Getting stuck in routines, allowing yourself to get caught up in negativity, or focusing on what matters *least* can begin to dim the light of your initial excitement. We sincerely believe maintaining balance in your life will sustain high levels of enthusiasm! A balanced educator can find the miracle in the mundane. For example, picture marveling at a sunrise—simply because you don't take it for granted. You seek it, find honor in its presence, and marvel in the moment. Translate that to other areas of your life: celebrating with a student who finally accesses learning in a deep and meaningful way, or instead of rushing to your next obligation, fully taking in the moment as your child places her arms around your neck, nuzzles up close, and whispers, "I love you." A balanced educator is able to engage with enthusiasm in all of these monotonous, yet miraculous, moments.

Visualize the version of you thriving in enthusiasm—when enthusiasm has seeped from your pores into the world around you. Or think about someone whose enthusiasm is inspiring. Enthusiasm is absolutely contagious, but a lack of it can also be. No student wants to sit in a classroom with a teacher that seems miserable with their job. Likewise, staff and students deserve to have a principal that leads with excitement. The vibes you put out deeply affect your classroom/school's culture. Being a balanced educator allows you to vibe out enthusiasm daily.

Balanced educators are enthusiastic people because they are fulfilled in all aspects of their lives: Their passions are electrified, they are immersed in each moment, they develop and maintain strong relationships personally and professionally, they are reflective and knowledgeable about their current state of balance in any area, and they transform themselves when needed. For all these reasons, balanced educators thrive with enthusiasm and impact those around them. Additionally, they can take a hit from any angle, recover quickly, and can approach problems with optimism.

No student wants to sit in a classroom with a teacher that seems miserable with their job.

#BalanceLAP

Approaching each of your roles with enthusiasm makes an incredible difference in the way you see tasks. Consider how easy it is to engage enthusiastically in the aspects of your position you are highly passionate about. A truly balanced educator can approach the tasks she's less passionate about with similar enthusiasm.

Sarah. As an instructional leader at the high-school level, I am extremely passionate about removing barriers to learning for our students. Give me an opportunity to engage in a solution-driven process for student learning, and my enthusiasm cannot be doused. When I am in balance, my enthusiasm shines even brighter, and I can even do the less attractive pieces of my job—like discipline or managerial tasks—without an internal groan. However, when balance is off, my enthusiasm is dimmed in my most passionate spaces because I cannot reconcile what I am currently doing versus where I feel my energies should be placed. For example, when I have not seen my children and husband much, I find it challenging to be enthusiastic about being at a board meeting, an athletic event, music concert, or parent-teacher conference. Those pieces begin to feel taxing and less important. Likewise, being with my children and husband at the cost of interactions with students and their families can also be stress inducing when I am out of balance. ■

It is hard to immerse yourself in any one space when you feel guilty for not balancing personal with positional. Additionally, your mental state might be dampened when not in balance because you have not taken the opportunity to grow professionally or have neglected what fuels your passions. There is nothing better than having an energy flow providing support and buoyancy so we can engage enthusiastically with people in all aspects of our lives.

Treasures from the Deep: Being a #JoyfulLeader

Bethany Hill, lead learner, Cabot, Arkansas

Joyful people ooze with enthusiasm. Ever been accused of being too enthusiastic? Too joyful? Too happy? Criticism like this can cut to the core and cause us to question ourselves. I have experienced this form of judgment, and allowed it to steal my joy. The opinions of someone else led me to consider sharing less and blending in more. In fact, I was so impacted by the criticism, I almost stepped away from who I am. Thankfully, a supportive group of friends helped me realize I needed to keep "doing me"! Part of balancing is surrounding ourselves with people who believe in us. I learned this valuable lesson from a hurtful experience, and it made me stronger.

Enthusiastic people tend to express excitement consistently and authentically! Some see this as a negative trait—as over-the-top, self-promoting, too transparent, or even fake. Can you believe it? But authentic enthusiasm comes from passion and joy for influencing others. One cannot fake it! Do we have moments where we feel deflated, exhausted, and even negative? Of course we do! Balanced leaders will overcome the negative feelings through seeking joy from others, reminding themselves of what is truly important, and sometimes saying "no!" Enthusiasm is the heart of influence: If we don't share our joy for what we do and who we are, we will never reach our true potential to impact the world around us.

Set Sail

- What does enthusiasm look like for you personally? How do you display it in your profession and at home?

- What is your current state of enthusiasm for your profession? Relationships in your life? How can you increase it even higher?

- Are you struggling to maintain enthusiasm at work or home? If so, what might be holding you back, and how can you address this with action or assistance?

Tweet it out with #BalanceLAP.

SECTION TWO
FINDING YOUR COMPASS

Let your heart be your
compass, your mind your
map, your soul your guide...
and you will never get lost.
—Angie Karan

All navigators rely upon a compass at some point. Over time, the tool has evolved from locating the direction of course based upon the position of the sun to a handheld mechanism fueled by gravity to digital tools that point us north. The key to balancing like a pirate is being able to define the directions, much like a compass. In this case, we are not talking about "never eat soggy wheat." The directions housed within *Balance Like a Pirate* contain a quartet of Ps: *personal, positional, professional, passions.*

In this section, we will define the balance quadrants in great detail, sharing with you personal stories of navigating to balance ourselves in these areas as well as the challenges we have faced and hope you can avoid.

We are completely certain that you all have your own stories of trial and triumph in seeking this elusive balance. Please keep in mind that seeking the balance is key, and little and large successes are found in the striving.

By the end of this section, you will have a great idea regarding which direction you will need to focus upon to chart your course to a more balanced version of yourself.

CALIBRATE

We are beautiful souls on a complicated journey.
—Sarah Johnson

When we tell others we are writing a book on balance, they quickly respond with eye rolls, sighs, or even laughter with statements like: *Life is never balanced, who really has it all?* Or, *Good luck with that!*

If you are looking for perfection in all areas of life, stop reading. If you were hoping to read a book by three people who have it all figured out, you might want to return it right now. We wrote this book to demystify the unicorn called "balance." Balance isn't about having it all, and it certainly isn't about reaching a final destination. Balance is a process—an opportunity to continually reflect on goals for our personal life, our positions, our profession, and our passions. Striving for balance isn't a means to an end; at no time will you feel you've arrived. But as in other aspects of your life, the value isn't in the destination—it is in the journey. Many of you have likely reached a point in your life where you do *not* want it all, but you *do* want a rich life, full of deep interactions, long-lasting memories, and opportunities to follow your personal and professional calling.

> Owning our story can be hard but not nearly as difficult as spending our lives running from it. Embracing our vulnerabilities is risky but not nearly as dangerous as giving up on love and belonging and joy—the experiences that make us the most vulnerable. Only when we are brave enough to explore the darkness will we discover the infinite power of our light.
>
> —Brené Brown

In Section One, we focused on the dynamic and different facets of balance using the acronym PIRATE. Section Two helps shape your course of action by setting intentional directions. Just like a compass leads you to a destination, the Four Quadrants of Balance help you identify areas of strength, areas of growth, and possible barriers to staying on course.

Priority over Preference

If you take only one idea from this book, we strongly encourage you to understand there are times you must select *priority over preference* in order to maintain balance. We know people are in constant conflict between what is urgent and what is important. To maintain balance, you will have to learn to always choose priority. However, this does *not* mean we must sacrifice any of our priorities or preferences in our balanced quadrants. Instead, it means we must approach those various parts of our lives differently.

Sarah. Running is one of my passions and vital to my personal balance. My running streak has survived since July 2014 because, fortunately, I understand there are times when I must choose the priority for the day over my preference. But this doesn't mean I completely give up my preference—I just have to adjust it. For example, I absolutely prefer to run in the morning for a myriad of reasons. However, to choose priority over preference *and* keep this passion in my balance quadrant, I may have to run at night or may only run one mile because my schedule does not allow for more. I've learned to select priority over the preference, but I never sacrifice the passions keeping me balanced. ■

In this section you will dig into the Four Quadrants of Balance, each representing a different aspect of your life. While it is impossible to maintain equilibrium between the quadrants, the goal is to have some activities in each quadrant at all times. In different seasons of life or for certain periods of time, one quadrant might require more of your time, energy, and attention than another. For example, "back to school" is a busy and stressful time for educators. You may not have as much time to read professional books or eat meals with your family since evening conferences fill your calendar. However, using the personal quadrant, you can still identify meaningful ways to connect with your family: Take a walk, or read for pleasure before you head to bed.

We've given you a brief description of each quadrant as a short introduction before we define them in greater detail and share stories and cautions with you in the following chapters. As we mentioned earlier, we want to emphasize balance is so much more than work and life. We are complex beings with a lot of energy and incredible amounts of potential to thrive!

Personal

This quadrant is about wellness in mind, body, and spirit. Within this space, you must consider mindfulness, self-care, and overall health. Very importantly, this quadrant also contains people and relationships—especially family and friends.

Professional

In this space you put forth energies to developing in your field of expertise, including learning and growing your professional learning network. In this quadrant, you might be going through coursework, reading, writing, and even presenting to other educators. We must always be involved in this space if we are to be lifelong learners.

Positional

Most often thought of as *work*, this is the space where your "titles" live. In this quadrant, you focus upon the job title you hold and the roles and responsibilities tied to it. This quadrant is most popular among the workaholics, and too often, the other three quadrants are at the mercy of this beast. But the good news is a process exists for addressing the addiction, and margin *can* be found, but we must seek it intentionally.

Passions

The best version of *you* is lying dormant in this space, waiting to be unleashed. We most often neglect this quadrant because we are so busy with the other three; we put passions aside. In this space, the guitar you've been meaning to play is gathering dust, or the traveling you want to do has been postponed. These pieces of you must not be forgotten! Your passions are what make you unique; they transcend all your titles from home and work to get down to the bare bones of you. Keep your fire burning. Keep the flames ignited.

I never lose—I either win or learn.
—Nelson Mandela

Remember, becoming balanced is a *process*—not a race. It isn't a game, and you are not a loser. Each day gives you a new opportunity to try again. As you will hear throughout the stories shared by other educators, perfection is not the focus.

As we've noted before, people often think of balance in two parts: work and life. But we believe in a deeper and richer framework, placing the priority on four areas of life. Journey with us as we explore those quadrants deeper. Open your mind and heart and be prepared to *Balance Like a PIRATE*!

Set Sail

- When was the last time you fed a passion of yours? What was it, and how long ago?

- Do you have a passion you have refused to let go or a passion you have missed and want to reclaim?

- Which quadrant do you think might be lacking the most attention in your life currently? Consider why this might be.

Tweet it out with #BalanceLAP.

PERSONAL

I don't have to chase extraordinary moments to
find happiness—it's right in front of me if I'm
paying attention and practicing gratitude.
—Brené Brown

Your level of success rarely exceeds your level
of personal development, because success is
something you attract by the person you become.
—Hal Elrod

What you consider personally important makes up a significant portion of your life. While people characterize "personal" as the life in work-life balance, it is essential to define what is important to us personally. People are most of what constitute the personal quadrant. When considering this quadrant, factor in your spouse, children, parents, siblings, friends, neighbors, and community.

But personal also involves a focus on self-care, a component we tend to neglect. Consider what you need to be present physically, mentally, emotionally, and spiritually. No matter how you characterize personal life, we believe it is exceptionally important. Without a healthy focus on this space, the rest of the quadrants fall apart.

Self-care is a vital part of our personal life we want to highlight more deeply. We want to delineate that focusing on self-care is different from a focus on self. Many educators believe in "servant leadership" as a pillar philosophy and recoil at the idea of selfishness. We believe that self-care is not selfish, and in fact, being healthy allows us to be more selfless. Our experiences, as well as plenty of research, support the idea that your cup is most full when you live a life poured

> # We believe that self-care is not selfish, and in fact, being healthy allows us to be more selfless.
>
> #BalanceLAP

out, so service to others is very important. However, burnout is a very real concern for educators, and you can be most at risk when you do not prioritize your own self-care. When you give to others endlessly without concern for your own well-being, you run the very real risk of temporary or permanent breakdown in your physical, mental, emotional, and/or spiritual health. We understand this very well. All three of us have very real examples of how we have sacrificed self-care and found ourselves broken. We also believe you understand this concept, but worry you sacrifice your personal quadrant the most and then find yourself bereft in imbalance.

Humans are social creatures and hold many personal titles such as child, spouse, sibling, cousin, friend, or family member. With each moniker, another person or group of people is tied to you in meaningful ways. When you consider the number of people in your life with whom you have deep connections and the amount of hours in each day, keeping those connections can be a challenge. Over the years, we have had countless discussions about how we keep our personal lives surviving and try to figure out ways to help them thrive. For us, our families tend to be our focus, and we are very mindful of the impact our positional and professional lives might have on our spouses and children. However, we also acknowledge friendships have suffered in the prioritization process. We really enjoy spending time with friends and within social circles, and a focus on these is necessary to balance this quadrant for us.

Navigating the Course

Personal Wellness

Sarah. I am not a lifelong runner. Prior to a few years ago, my exercise patterns consisted of many two- to three-week stints, trailing off without any lasting effect. When I started my running streak on July 11, 2014, my life was at a crossroads. I had just hit "submit" on an application for a new position, just meeting the deadline. My principal position at that time required I travel approximately forty minutes one way every day, and with a five-year-old and a three-year-old, the enormity of my responsibilities was becoming mind numbing to balance. Pressure was beginning to break me, and I was finding few outlets to refill and restore myself—at least none healthy for my family.

Running began as a way to find space for myself where there was none—time away to just think and be me. Out on the pavement, I wasn't required to be anyone other than *me*: Sarah. Not mom, wife, principal, friend, daughter, or sister. Just Sarah. I had forgotten who she was and when I was running, I spent so much time in my head, it was impossible to not begin to see myself clearly again.

I started out small—small but disciplined steps such as getting out every day, but allowing myself to run/walk. There was no expectation for length of time or mileage because I wasn't tracking either. I simply wanted to be out of my house, away from others, and in my own space to process. I spent many months reflecting on current reality as I ran. As my physical strength was building up, my mental and spiritual stamina were also increasing.

By the end of year one, I had run through an incredible amount of personal and professional turmoil: from losing my brother to suicide to another brother being incarcerated. My family was devastated. My closest circle was in turmoil from the utter lack of balance, and home was not a refuge. My marriage was broken from my focusing on my position and falling into the wrong line of thinking regarding what I needed to keep going. Professionally, the school to where I had transitioned was experiencing a dramatic cultural upheaval, which culminated at the end of the year with a well-publicized student walk-out and demonstrations on school grounds. I found myself caught in the midst of a pending lawsuit and a season of turnover from staff to board members. To say my first year in this new position was a challenge is a severe understatement.

The road and my running PLN became my refuge to get me through the year. Through them I began to think differently about running and about my ability. I ran a 5K with a friend and jumped jubilantly over the finish line, having never run a formal race. My time was nothing like I was capable of at the time (I was built for speed in those days), but my goal was to finish with my friend, and the experience lifted me.

In year two, I continued to run, learn terrain, and test my limits—finding I had fewer than I thought. At the same 5K race I was simply happy to finish last year, I ran hard and placed third overall and second in my age group, giving me a taste of internal competition. I started thinking this running thing I did for myself might be something I was also good at. Work stress was increasing, family life stress was decreasing, and my PLN connection was thriving. In May 2016, during the second year of my streak, I ran my first half-marathon with my PLN, composed of four other principals, including my fellow coauthors, Jessica Cabeen and Jessica Johnson! Their encouragement helped me stretch my mind, as I had never run so many miles before.

A few weeks after the ticker turned on my two-year streak, Adam Welcome, coauthor of *Kids Deserve It*, changed my life. He had been encouraging me to run a marathon with him and another principal, Jay Posick. Though I had run a half-marathon, I still did not believe I could do the full 26.2 miles. Adam and Jay had been talking about running a marathon together for a while, and our Voxer group "Endurance Educators" encouraged them from afar. In August of that year, Adam let us know he could not do the Marine Corps Marathon in October, and asked if anybody would take his place. I knew his spot was for me, but sat on the decision for a few days.

With fewer weeks than are normally desirable to train, I made the decision to run a destination marathon with Jay. Up to this point, running had been a space only for myself, and this experience would grow me in multiple ways. Adam took on the role of coach over Voxer, providing tips for eating and listening to my body in training. "Respect the marathon," was the mantra I heard in his California accent during my training.

Running the marathon was an incredible experience. Having Jay, a veteran marathon runner and one whose streak I will never be able to catch (he has run every single day since August 1987!), was inspiring, uplifting, and instrumental in my completion of this first marathon. I will never regret or forget my memories from this experience!

During the third year of my running streak, I completed another marathon in May 2017, where I achieved my personal record ("PR" in running lingo). Today, I run without earbuds, listening for my direction, trusting in the deep spiritual connection I have forged over the miles and years of reflection.

This running chapter in my life has been balancing. I have learned through this journey, new phases and growth are always present. I now see running as a gift and a space allowing me to be present, focused on my spiritual, emotional, and physical health. The very act of choosing to run daily, whether one mile or 26.2 miles, has literally transformed my life and contributed to my current state of balance and shine—something I had not thought possible back in 2015. As I have devoted time to this personal passion, I have become a better leader, mother, wife, sister, and friend. I am much more centered when I return from a run, and my energy levels are on point every day from my morning endorphin burst. I didn't realize what I had been missing until I tipped my balance back on keel again. ■

Jessica. In the past, when I thought about personal wellness—well, truthfully, I really didn't think about it. Personal wellness was on the bottom rung of my "to-do" list. I prioritized others before myself, and my health paid dearly. In college I ate terribly, I never exercised, and my sleep habits weren't great. As I moved into my first job, I learned quickly I didn't even have a hobby; I had just plowed through college in four and a half years and didn't know how to slow down!

My first "run" was with my brother. We signed up for a 5K, and I think I was three blocks into it before I had to stop. I was thirty pounds heavier than I am now and completely out of shape. I was also less than fifteen years away from the age my mother was when she was diagnosed with breast cancer. This was the final wake-up call I needed.

I signed up with the YMCA in Mason City, Iowa, and started taking classes and using the treadmill. I actually started eating *meals*— before 3:00 in the afternoon—and watched what I was eating (less fast food and more fresh food). I started going to sleep and waking up at a regular time. The results? I felt better about myself and felt healthier as well. Since then, I have continued to find ways to challenge my personal well-being by cleansing my diet two times per year, changing my exercise routines (yoga, TRX, cycling, running, walking) during the year and, most recently, eating more vegan and vegetarian throughout the week.

I did experience some roadblocks to my personal wellness, the first being guilt I felt about putting myself first during the first few months after I had my son. Before kids I had a lot of free time to run, bike, take exercise classes, and still have time to work and enjoy time with my husband. Then Kenny came along, and I felt I was being selfish if I took any time for me. But over the past twelve years, he has been my joy and become a balancer for my health. I found if I was tired, sad, crabby, ornery, or even a little "off," a quick walk or run really changed my mood and made me a better mom. I learned thirty to forty-five minutes for myself in the morning meant I had more patience for my son and spouse. Plus, I felt better about myself. My husband also saw this change in me and continues to encourage me to take time for myself (at times poking the "bear" in me, "Honey, you sure you don't need to go for a run?!?!?"). Now my boys come and cheer me on during my races, and I can model for them they have to take care of themselves first in order to be good for others. ■

Another potential roadblock is procrastination. Making excuses like "I will run tomorrow . . . start a diet next week . . . sleep in one more day" can be the biggest challenge to making a change in your personal well-being. But you can't learn from something until you start it. Maybe you need to find an accountability partner, buy a new pair of shoes, or preplan your meals on the weekend so you have no excuses on Monday morning. *You are worth* doing whatever is needed to take care of yourself! So stop delaying and put your health and personal well-being first.

11. While developing healthy habits for personal wellness often makes the three of us think of running, for many, general health and well-being is even more basic. In my early years as an administrator, I went all in with a servant-leadership mindset, truly giving everything I had from early morning until late night. I applied a "people during the day, paperwork at night" mindset, took on tasks to make others' work easier, and poured myself into others—all at the expense of my own personal health and well-being. I never made appointments for yearly doctor or dentist visits, and I certainly wasn't doing much else to take care of myself.

I shouldn't have been surprised when I ended up in the emergency room multiple times due to work stress taking over my life. I had kidney stones from fueling my days with Dr. Pepper. Another time I had what seemed to be a stroke, though they determined it was likely due to anxiety and stress. My bad habit of clenching my jaw during times of stress and frustration landed me in the emergency room when my TMJ seized up so much I temporarily lost hearing in my right ear and could hardly open my mouth to eat! I had to go to physical therapy for weeks before I could eat normally again.

It took me years to truly understand it is not selfish to put myself first. Todd Whitaker's well-known phrase, "When the principal sneezes, the whole school catches a cold," became a daily reminder for me in many ways. I had always interpreted this as a call to lead with a positive attitude to set the tone for staff and students. But I realized it was also connected to my personal well-being:

- If I am sick, it is okay to take a sick day. Potentially passing my illness to others isn't fair, and I'm useless when I'm sick.
- I have to take care of myself first before I can take care of so many others. When I overextend myself, I am no good to anyone! ■

When considering your level of balance with the personal quadrant, you must also review wellness. Stress is a debilitating reality of an educator's career. While some stress is healthy for your brain, overloads of it with no mitigating behaviors can have a significant negative impact on wellness. The research on stress and its impact on personal wellness are both clear and frightening. For example,

- Multiple studies have shown sudden emotional stresses—especially anger—can trigger heart attacks, arrhythmias, and even sudden death. Although this happens mostly in people who already have heart disease, some people don't know they have a problem until acute stress causes a heart attack or something worse.
- Work-related stress is associated with burnout, job dissatisfaction, and physical as well as mental health outcomes.
- A 2015 study reported by statista.com identifies that high stress can weaken the immune system and cause exhaustion in the body. Work is one of the most common sources of stress for adults. This study identified the following reported symptoms or unhealthy behaviors due to stress among adults in the United States:
  - 37 percent reported feeling irritable or angry
  - 42 percent reported feeling nervous or anxious
  - 37 percent reported feeling depressed or sad
  - 33 percent reported feeling constantly worried

- An informal study conducted by Jerry Murphy, former dean of the Harvard Graduate School of Education, revealed about school leaders:
  - 89 percent reported feeling overwhelmed
  - 84 percent reported neglecting to take care of themselves in the midst of stress
  - 80 percent reported scolding themselves when they performed less than perfectly

While the costs of stress and burnout are high and poor contributing habits are so deeply ingrained, you might think the solution would be complicated, right? Michael Hyatt says the cure for burnout culture is simple: Work less, rejuvenate more!

A focus on balance within this quadrant involves building healthy habits to impact your physical health, such as regular exercise and healthy eating. There is also an inclusion of mindful practices to help positively impact your mental and emotional well-being. Finally, don't forget your spiritual health. Regardless of your personal viewpoints, spiritual wellness transcending beyond but potentially including religion has a well-established impact on overall personal well-being. German philosopher Josef Pieper writes, "Leisure is only possible when we are at one with ourselves. We tend to overwork as a means of self-escape, as a way of trying to justify our existence."

If your humble side is still concerned about putting yourself first, reflect on this quote from Hal Elrod, author of *The Miracle Morning*: "Your level of success rarely exceeds your level of personal development, because success is something you attract by the person you become."

We fully believe this because we have each benefitted from carving out time for our own personal development—whether by reading books for our personal and professional growth, listening to podcasts to help us grow personally, or connecting with others.

Who you surround yourself with is also important to your personal growth. Author and motivational speaker Jim Rohn famously said, "You are the average of the five people you spend the most time with." We know children who surround themselves with positive people tend to make better life choices and, correspondingly, children who surround themselves with friends who tend to make poor choices can suffer a negative impact. Who do you surround yourself with at work and in your personal life? Do you spend time with positive people who hold the same passions as you, lift you up, hold you accountable, and inspire you? We have each found our professional PLN to be a tremendous encouragement in our personal lives as well, as we have branched into different social media groups focusing on personal areas of growth, in a Voxer group about running, another for an ongoing book-study discussion, and even a private Facebook group dedicated to time management and organization.

The bottom line is if we do not intentionally balance ourselves in our personal quadrant, we run a high risk of losing a lot. Families break apart, mental health crises occur, physical health declines, and our support networks flounder. Take it from us. We have been nearly sunk by the cannons in this space.

Cannonballs to Avoid

Attacks Threatening to Sink Your Personal Life Ship

Sarah. *Did he die?* was my gut reaction to the news that had just shattered the momentum of my day and stopped time. Mom said he hung himself last night. I stared at the carpet in my office but, even as my mind started folding inside itself to shield whatever part of my brain processes emotions, there remained the problem-solving administrator who felt she could find a sliver of hope in this information. We hung up, and I tried not to vomit. I don't know how long I sat in my office with all the fixtures swirling around me. Somehow, I managed to walk calmly to my superintendent's office to tell her the news, smiling at faces as I passed them, a mask plastered on my face. I recall promising her I would be back the next day. Formal teacher observations were to be completed, and I didn't want to let them down. It was a Tuesday, and my unrelenting calendar held no room for a personal tragedy.

But I did not return the next day. In fact, by the time my mind processed the fact that my oldest brother had ended his life by suicide, I didn't want to return. Ever.

As a leader, your emotional intelligence has a strong impact on how people will relate with you. Because you are in a field where you encounter people every day and every interaction counts, some of the most challenging times are when you become emotionally bankrupt. Educators are not superhuman. You will face personal tragedies and challenges threatening your ability to be present. How do you manage your emotions and the inner turmoil to be able to remain effective during these storms? I truly do not have an exact answer for you. All I can do is share how I came back from my own devastation.

Talk It Out

I began seeing a counselor, and over time, speaking the pain out loud and using strategies offered by the counselor began to help. Having a space to reveal my truths and the pain erupting inside me every day was essential. Keeping my grief and range of emotions that ebbed and flowed inside felt like a miracle, especially when I encountered others' pain. And for some reason, I encountered a lot more of others' pain in those subsequent months: students who had uncles and parents who had completed suicides, other students who were thinking of doing the same. Always through this, though, my exterior remained what was needed as a leader. Calm. Consoling. Empathetic. Inside, I felt I was drowning, spinning in the current of my own pain, loss, and questions. But talking through my pain with a stranger allowed me to give it over to someone who wouldn't hurt from the shared experience, and work through the guilt of not being a good enough reason to make my brother want to stick around and my overwhelming sense of lack of control. Talking it out allowed me to process and cope, which helped me maintain my important presence at school.

Reach Out

During this time, my other five siblings were my refuge. When I returned to school the following Monday, more students than ever seemed to come into my office and reveal their own painful stories with me as a result of my rooting out the source of their poor behavior choices. We all cope differently with these struggles, after all. I had to dig my nails into my hands to listen with empathy. Thankfully, my siblings were always a text away. I have since learned that engaging in our cathartic group texts cost me some professional credibility based on appearances at that time. I admittedly had my cell phone at the ready to receive their messages, but I believe being in touch with them got me through those hardest days. They were outside my job, but inside my pain.

Treat Yourself Gently

I had to forgive myself for falling short of the expectations my calendar represented. The district expectation at the time was all licensed staff were on the evaluation cycle, a very daunting task, challenging even in normal circumstances. Add this to my complete lack of desire to care about anything due to the ensuing depression, and I had a recipe for a nasty self-loathing cycle. As hard as it was, I forgave myself for missing deadlines here and there, chose not to over commit, and spoke honestly. The challenge from that gentleness to self came with the fact that not everyone else forgave me. Truthfully, I probably retained my equanimity too well at work; many people forgot I was fragile. Upon reflection, I lost an opportunity to build trust with my staff by being more outwardly vulnerable and helping them understand leaders also struggle. I was too focused on what I thought they needed from me instead of what I needed from them.

Find The Spaces Where Joy Exists

I sought refuge in the choir room and during lunch hours! During this painful experience, sometimes encounters with other people could chafe. This was problematic as a leader with so many interactions. I found going into the choir room fed my joy at work and allowed me to recover from grief for those few minutes. Engaging informally with students during their lunch breaks also allowed me to focus on them and find joy in their relaxed presence. These interactions fed my purpose and reminded me why I needed to stay focused and work through it, better equipping me to interact with all stakeholders directly when necessary.

Lean In

My network got me through these challenging times and other school-related challenges during the spring. When I removed myself from my situation to listen to others, I realized they faced struggles and challenges too. My world was small and important, but the greater world was large and connected. Jessica Johnson may never know how important our Voxer chats were during those times to keep me focused on the important work at school. Our connection allowed me to share the turmoil and challenges of a school day in a safe space with someone who understood. I continue to process, and there are always reminders and pain, but my connection to Jessica Cabeen and Jessica Johnson always provides an empathetic, nonjudgmental space when I experience a trigger. I will continue to lean in to them because I know I must to keep myself in balance.

Being mindful of where you are out of balance will help you counteract those times threatening to take you down. During my loss, I was truly the most unbalanced I have ever been in my life. I was not eating, sleeping well, or finding personal joys enough. My focus was on keeping it together positionally and finding my space within my family. I spent many days filling my siblings and parents, even neglecting my husband and children. I simply had nothing left over for several pretty dark weeks. Having the vulnerability to state this and correct it is what turned the balance back to center for me. It took time. In fact, we are still bouncing back, but as someone who has come through this level of off-balance, I can tell you it can and *will* be done.

I hope my story offers a beacon to you if you are facing similar challenges in life. Whether you are thrown off balance by loss from death, divorce, or something else, you are meant to hold pain and promise at the same time. If you choose vulnerability and action at pivotal moments, you won't sink. ■

Set Sail

- In what ways are you focusing on your own self-care? Is this a space needing attention?

- Commit to one way you will add focus on self-care daily (eating breakfast [or lunch] every day, walking for fifteen minutes each morning, meditating or writing in a journal for ten minutes a day).

Tweet it out with #BalanceLAP.

PROFESSIONAL

Never stop learning, because life never stops
teaching. A wise girl knows her limits,
a smart girl knows she has none.
—Marilyn Monroe

In the professional quadrant, the focus is on growing and learning from where you are currently. Going beyond taking additional coursework, professional learning may include regularly reading books, attending conferences, listening to webinars and podcasts, joining in on Twitter chats or Voxer discussion groups, etc. Educators only get better when they work with others. Think about it: Have you ever had an idea and someone offered suggestions, adding value to it? Professional growth includes creating—or expanding—your PLN, connecting with a teacher from a different school, grade level, or state. You could set up Google hangouts and create challenges between classrooms across the country, collaboratively planning without setting foot in the same room.

Letting It Go

Brené Brown's book *The Gifts of Imperfection* has such a powerful message, summed up in the subtitle: *Let Go of Who You Think You're Supposed to Be and Embrace Who You Are.* Brown is a well-known author, speaker, and research professor who has spent years studying courage, vulnerability, shame, and empathy. In her work, she clarifies the difference between *guilt* (a feeling about behavior or having done something wrong) and *shame* (feelings about self, worth, or not fitting in).

As an educator, spouse, parent, friend, etc. you may find it's easy to feel shame about not doing good enough or not being enough.

- If only I could lose ten pounds.
- I can't believe how awful my lesson was. What was I thinking?
- I just suck at this job! Why can't I raise any of our achievement scores?

When these kinds of thoughts pop in your head, they are rooted in shame. You're a super passionate educator constantly seeking to be better, or even striving for perfection, but it's an impossible feat, and it sabotages your true greatness and worth. As a result, you feel shame when you spend too much time beating yourself up. Mel Robbins, another well-known author and speaker, says, "If you're in your head, you're behind enemy lines." Ponder this a moment. When have you been behind enemy lines in your own thoughts or arguments with yourself?

If these types of negative, self-deprecating statements are part of the self-talk in your head, then the positive affirmations you wrote after reading Chapter Four are going to be critical for you. Revisit your affirmations now. Do you need to add any more to your list to make sure that when you are "in your head" that you are not "behind enemy lines"? Remember, the purpose of affirmations is to infuse your mind with positivity and intentionality, to retrain your brain to think positive instead of negative.

J. I am really good at giving educators the cliché advice "Don't take it personally." But I am terrible at following this recommendation myself. I'm sure you can relate. Constantly striving to be a better leader for our staff and students makes it nearly impossible for me *not* to take something personally. In the past, when I received staff feedback surveys about myself as an administrator and our school culture, I spent weeks depressed about myself as a leader, thinking of other job and career options. Seriously, I did this every year for probably four years, until I opened up to other administrators and learned they all get the same stinging feedback. *What?!* I was so relieved to realize I wasn't alone. And honestly, when I dug into the feedback, the painful comments were only a small percentage of the feedback, which meant I wasn't spending any time celebrating and appreciating the positive comments. ■

So what are you to do in moments of shame or when you're behind enemy lines inside your own head? *Let it go!* Seriously. Sing the song from *Frozen*. (Just kidding, it might not be your thing to enjoy singing for stress relief!) But when you're striving for balance, you have to let go of the negativity. Brown says you should recognize when you're in a spiral of shame and not take any action then. My physical reactions to shame are getting a flushed face and neck, getting sweaty, and screaming angry thoughts inside my head. During these moments I know I should *not* respond to "that" email or say out loud what I'm thinking. Instead, I close my laptop and walk away, or send a quick response saying I will have to get back to them and then go find my happy place. If I'm still in school, I go to the kindergarten classroom, or I wait until the end of the day and go for a run.

Navigating the Course

JJ. I have always loved learning and have continued to be a sponge, soaking up any new opportunity for learning. Ironically, when I decided to pursue a master's degree, I have to confess, it was ultimately to move up the salary schedule and I chose the administration path only because my colleagues were all joining a cohort together. I had no intentions of ever becoming a principal. Now that I have eleven years under my belt of loving my role as a school administrator, it was the best aimless career choice I made! While I learned a great deal in my master's coursework and became inspired to lead, I do feel that I have learned even more from building a PLN on Twitter that has deepened through discussions and personal connections on Voxer. I truly mean it when I say that I could not do my job if I didn't have these connections—I was literally at the point of quitting during my first year as principal until I got connected on Twitter.

My journey started small, just following a handful of other principals and not even engaging with them, just observing and getting re-energized from the ideas being shared. After getting a better handle on what this Twitter thing was, I started to reach out to ask for more information about someone's tweet, engage in a live Twitter chat, or send a personal message to inquire for advice about a situation. Even though I was the only elementary principal in my small, rural district with no similar colleagues to connect with, I was building a vast network of colleagues on Twitter and took time to know what each person's area of expertise was. This allowed me to reach out to Chad Kafka (@ChadKafka) for any questions on Google apps because he was a Google certified expert, Curt Rees (@CurtRees) to pick his brain about RTI because his school was recognized at the state level for being a model RTI school, Amber Teamann (@8Amber8) for her constant sharing of ways to integrate technology, and Pernille Ripp

(@pernilleripp) for her passion in literacy as the creator of the Global Read Aloud and an avid blogger known for her deep reflection on doing what is best for students, even when it means breaking the mold. My list could go on and on with those that I have built connections with on Twitter, but my point is, I created an incredible toolbox of resources to turn to that both inspire and refuel my passion for my profession each and every day.

When conversations needed to go deeper than typing on Twitter, we moved to a different venue so we could actually engage in face-to-face discussions in Skype or Google Hangout. With some of the members of my PLN, our conversations continued so deeply that we decided to share our passion with others and began the writing process together. Without even meeting in person, I am fortunate to have written three books with different coauthors, all via Google docs and Google hangout.

The principal role is extremely isolating, but my PLN helps me through it. Had I had a PLN as a teacher, I think I would have been a much better teacher due to the wealth of ideas and reflections being shared publicly today that just weren't there prior to social media, blogs, and podcasts. I waiver on my aspirations of whether or not to pursue a doctorate program due to the high cost and the fact that I feel I have learned more from my PLN than I did in my master's program courses! ◼

- **Cultivate a PLN.** Gone are the days of working in isolation. Whether your role is the only position like yours in your school or there are multiple colleagues in the same role in your building, our work can be isolating, but it does not have to be. Get connected to other educators in your field so you can continue to surround yourself with others to learn and grow with. You can build a PLN by connecting with others on Twitter, LinkedIn, or Facebook and can have further in-depth conversations with those educators on Voxer. Get over the weird feeling of not really knowing "in person" who is on the other side of the Internet and be open to the possibility of learning from other educators across your state, country, and world.

- **Continue your own learning.** Don't be the type of educator who only learns if it's a required training or necessary credits to renew licensure. There are so many opportunities to continue your own professional learning, which can reignite your passion for your work, make you more effective, and cause you to love your job even more. Search online for a topic you want to know more about and you are bound to find blogs, books, podcasts, or webinars to fuel your learning. The professional conferences you could attend are endless, depending on the cost options available to you. One of our favorites is the What Great Educators Do Differently conference, which has been spreading across the United States thanks to the work of Jimmy Casas and Jeff Zoul. If cost is a roadblock for you, then look for your nearest EdCamp, a free "unconference" that empowers educators to find sessions that meet their needs. As you attend conferences, continue to build your PLN by adding people you meet in Twitter or Voxer. Conferences become even more exciting when you know ahead of time if someone in your PLN is going to be there; it is fun to meet someone "in real life" that you have been learning from in Twitter chats!

- **Go to school, go back to school, or set your own course for ongoing learning.** Whether you need to continue to take classes to maintain your licensure, move up the salary schedule, or want to pursue a higher degree, continuing your coursework is a great way to grow as a professional. We encourage you to not just pick the easiest online class to knock off credits that you "have to have," but instead select a course that is truly going to meet your professional needs to continue to grow and thrive in your current role or the role you are pursuing to move into. Maybe you're a teacher aspiring to be an administrator, or a teacher deeply concerned about students and feel you'd make a great school counselor, or a teacher that wants to move into an instructional coach role to have a broader impact, choosing the appropriate program and courses to do so will be important for your professional journey.

Focusing upon this professional quadrant means truly embracing a lifelong learning philosophy and being a person who challenges yourself to grow intrinsically. This quadrant is different from positional because educators can gain a position title but stop learning after they're hired, becoming stagnant in the level of professional knowledge and connection. Positions and titles certainly signify professionalism, but they do not signify professional learning. Growing professionally is up to you in all phases of your career and life.

Cannonballs to Avoid

I don't have it all—but I have everything I need.

You make tons of decisions every day—from what to wear, to what to make for dinner, to how to have a difficult conversation with a teacher, parent, or student. With each decision, you have the opportunity to:

- Reflect on what went well and what could have gone differently (Option A); *or*
- Beat yourself up and down over it (Option B). (While I [Jessica]) like to think I always take Option A, I know I don't.)

The decisions you make as educators have a direct impact on the lives around you. Sometimes those decisions create happiness and other times hurt feelings. Regardless of the emotional outcomes of others, calibrating your own emotional response is what stabilizes your own daily emotions. If you hop onto others' emotional roller-coasters, you are in for an exhausting and time-wasting emotional up-and-down, completely out of your control.

Jessica. I have learned two key ways to keep others' emotions in check and to not let them disrupt my day.

- Reframe.
- Is the glass half full or half empty?
- Life is ten percent what happens to you and ninety percent how you respond to it.
- You can change the world by changing how you see it.
- We may not be able to direct the wind, but we can adjust our sails.

Do these adages sound familiar? They are all somewhat common sayings to remind people they have the power to choose their perspective. Maybe you've adopted one of these to help you reframe your own thoughts when needed. The power of positivity isn't just cliché; people give up when they don't have the optimism, positivity, or belief to keep moving forward. If you can make it a habit to reframe difficult situations, you can continue to move forward on your path.

I admit it. The year we focused on improvisation in our professional development, I was a skeptic. How could changing my mind-set from one of fear to one of discovery really change how I see the world? After a few months, though, I changed some key routines, significantly changing my outlook.

For example, I started using one of my favorite activities I learned from Brave New Workshop called "What's in the Box?" My partner and I took turns giving each other an imaginary box. When I took the box from my partner, I asked her, "What's in the box?" During the first few turns, the "gift" was something desirable (i.e., a week of paid vacation, a nice necklace, dinner out), and I described my ideal or picture of the desirable gift. My partner would then add more detail about why I might need the item and then I added more description. Later, the gift becomes something "negative" (an additional course assignment, rotten food, Internet down during testing, flat tire) and we still had to find the "positive" in the gift. Using the idea of this activity, I could look at any situation and find the good in it.

Around the same time we started using improv in our professional development, I purchased a Panda Planner, a planner with a daily reflection prompting me to identify three things I was looking forward to during the day. Using my newly found improvisational skills, I was able to reframe my day before it even started. For example:

Activity on My Schedule	How I Reframed It
Four-hour admin meeting	I am excited to have the opportunity to connect with other leaders in the district to have deeper conversations about our students and schools.
Meeting with an upset parent	I am looking forward to the opportunity to hear concerns and come up with a way to help support families and students in our school.
Two teachers out and only one substitute available	Today I can build upon our teamwork, bringing in key teachers to help problem solve the shortage for today, and also create scenarios for future shortages.

In *The Carpenter* by Jon Gordon, he states, "Your optimism today will determine your level of success tomorrow." By practicing reframing every day, I began to see "challenges" in my daily schedules as opportunities to see things in a different way. I no longer went to work dreading meetings, but I drove into the parking lot with the silver lining visible from the outset. ■

Turn to Your PLN

]]. My favorite funny video clip is "Principal Meltdown." Each time I watch Principal Wilson lose his marbles for his entire school to hear, I laugh so hard I cry. Seriously, you must stop reading right now, go to YouTube, search "Principal Meltdown," and enjoy two minutes of crazy humor. Sometimes when I am having a really bad day at work, I close my door and watch this video because laughter is the best medicine. Plus, it reminds me even though I feel like yelling at everyone who is driving me crazy, I would look just like him! There are better ways to handle my frustrations.

While Principal Wilson's meltdown is fictional for a commercial, I feel this way when my ship is sinking. He wasn't losing his temper because someone parked in his spot; the parking spot was just the final straw for him. Obviously, he had been keeping inside a lot of things that were bothering him and building up his frustration to the point he just let it all blow when someone parked in his spot. I'd like to think his embarrassing (and probably career-ending if in real life) explosion could have been prevented by venting to a PLN or a trusted colleague, or having a Voxer group to support and encourage him through his daily frustrations. While many connected educators converse daily in Twitter chats or tweet out ideas to share with others, the frustrations that you want to hash out with someone who will understand is not something that should be done publicly on Twitter. Sure, you could send a private direct message to someone, but we advocate the use of Voxer for the days you need to lean in to your PLN on a difficult day. We are each in a number of different groups on Voxer, each with a different purpose. We don't always keep up with them fully, but since we do spend enough time in certain groups, we know which group would be the appropriate space to share a frustration or challenge we have encountered to seek advice, or just hear encouraging words from someone else who has likely already been there. But you can't just wait to get on Voxer until you've had a bad day; you need to get connected on it now and start building your PLN so you will know whom to turn to when you need it most. Someone else who will likely be grateful for your PLN is your spouse—because you can get your venting out before going home and then enjoy your family time. ▪

Set Sail

- Do you have a strong PLN to turn to for advice, encouragement, or a push when you need to grow? If not, spend time thinking about how you can cultivate one. For starters, consider joining our #BalanceLAP Voxer group. Follow the hashtag on Twitter, follow some people, connect over the balance topic, and move from there!

- How positive are you? How would those closest to you answer that question about you? If you let cannonballs take you down, then begin a practice of reframing. When you catch yourself thinking negatively about a situation, push "pause" and think about how you can look at it through a different lens to reframe your situation with positivity.

- What books have you wanted to read, but have been putting off? Make a list of them and set goals to read them.

- Are you an avid reader or maybe even a published author already? Consider how you might grow professionally by presenting on your topic, spreading your message further, or even spreading someone else's message by providing a review of their work on Amazon or Goodreads.

Tweet it out with #BalanceLAP.

Positional

Success leaves clues. Connect with
others to learn from their path.
—Ken Williams

Boundaries are what you create
and what you allow.
—Dr. Henry Cloud

Earlier we referred to the positional quadrant as a "beast"—with all the other quadrants potentially being at its mercy. This is because it tends to be all consuming—the quadrant most often tipping our balance out of kilter. We love being educators. We know you love being educators. And like us, you probably feel called to be an educator. However, there is a crisis in the calling of education, made clear in the statistics:

- Between forty and fifty percent of new teachers leave education during their first seven years.
- Teacher attrition in the United States has grown by fifty percent since 1992.
- On average, the length of a principal's tenure at a given school is three to four years.
- While a principal's short tenure may mean leaving one school to lead another, the turnover of leadership adversely affects schools.

Both teachers and principals become more effective as they gain experience, but obviously not if they burn out and possibly leave the profession. Teaching is hard work. Add on extra duties, meetings, ongoing professional learning outside of the school day, likely bringing home lesson planning and grading work to tackle after your own children are in bed, and teaching is an almost impossibly hard job. A principal's day is rarely ever the same, due to the nature of the job of responding to the needs of students, staff, parents, and community. The hours are unforgiving, often starting early in the morning and lasting into the evening, when sporting events (especially at the secondary level, the parents and community expect to see the principal there), school board meetings, or other school functions are scheduled. All of these can cut into personal family time, leaving you feeling tremendous guilt for spending more evenings at school than at home.

While the statistics and reality of the role can be disheartening, you may be encouraged to know it can get better with time. One study found the probability of principals leaving their current school increases each year for the first five years of tenure within a school. However, it decreases for principals with tenures of at least six years.

So, essentially, if you can survive the five-year-long crash course without sinking, you can make it for the long haul!

But wait. You don't want to *survive* this profession. By definition, surviving means you are just barely living, despite your conditions. If you are only surviving, you are not achieving your potential in your personal and professional life. Likely those around you at school and at home see you as drained and negative, and you are not having the impact on others you dreamed of when you decided to become an educator.

This positional quadrant encompasses the variety of titles you hold within any particular organization—instructional leader, lead learner, team leader, department chair, teacher—and their associated responsibilities. This is in addition to the personal titles you wear every day outside of your profession. We acknowledge this quadrant can evolve often and can also be the dominant one when it comes to getting off balance. The positional quadrant is what most people characterize as the "work" aspect of work-life balance. This quadrant also includes everything associated with our main job titles, as well as all other "duties as assigned." The positional quadrant can also include any roles you have outside your paid position (volunteer, civic duties, etc.)

Think about what your position means to you in the larger picture of your whole life. You can lose your position for a myriad of reasons, and if you fasten your ship to your position and it goes down, you are sunk. Additionally, it is sobering though important to consider how an intense focus on this quadrant, without factoring in the other three quadrants, can lead to devastating loss of what you value most, including your family, passions, and professional pursuits.

We continually advocate for educators to be connected and we personally enjoy the professional learning gained from Twitter, Voxer, blogs, podcasts, and Facebook; however, we also realize that these platforms can also be distractors from work and personal or family time. We love the work that Cal Newport shares in his book *Deep Work: Rules for Focused Success in a Distracted World.* Newport writes, "To succeed with deep work, you must rewire your brain to be comfortable resisting distracting stimuli." Stimuli can include notifications from email, Twitter, Facebook, texts, Instagram, Snapchat, or any other phone app you are glued to during the day and night.

If you are in the "distraction" boat, then what about taking the notifications off your phone? You know where to find the app and can check it when you want to. But when notifications are enabled, the little red flag can distract you and cause unnecessary stress—especially if it has a large number on it. Consider how many times during the day that you check your phone notifications, whether at work or at home, and how many times are they pertinent to what you are currently doing versus just a distraction from where your focus should be? Did it matter that you checked it at that moment, or could life have gone on fine while waiting until a better time of the day to check in?

Jessica. If you are like me, you may even need some physical barriers between you and your device at any spare moment. During my morning walkthroughs, I usually leave my phone in my office. For twenty minutes each morning I need to be uninterrupted and focused, walking into each classroom to greet all the students and staff—not looking down at the newest notification popping up on my phone. Once you set the boundaries of turning off your phone or keeping your distance from it, you will be surprised how much mental time you free up. ■

Setting boundaries of work is important to separate the person from the position as well. Educators can be sidetracked by a new initiative, a new request or, as Todd Whitaker writes, a "new monkey." By establishing and sticking to goals and a plan, you have an easy out when anything new comes your way. Dr. Henry Cloud states in his book *Boundaries for Leaders,* "Boundaries are what you create and what you allow." Think about it. How often have you wanted to set the tone for a positive school culture or classroom, but when people criticize or complain, you allow it? Or what if your school mantra is "All Means All," but you hear a teacher say things about specific children certainly not aligned to the school vision? Just like in your classroom and family, don't create a rule or expectation if you yourself don't expect to follow it.

Jessica. After a number of years as a teacher, I had a challenging class I couldn't quite figure out, even though it was mid-year. Each day I came to school with a clean slate, but by lunchtime I felt defeated. I reflected on student behaviors, trying to identify what needed to change. Only after I figured out *I* needed to change—not my students—did things improve. I realized eating lunch with a group of adults who always complained about the school, their students, or their personal lives wasn't giving me the time I needed to regroup, refocus, and reflect on how to make positive changes for the rest of the day. After this, I started eating lunch in a different space, reading articles about ways to help students self-regulate better, and sometimes ate or went to recess with the students. This change in *my* behavior had a direct impact on how my classroom climate changed. ■

Regardless of what drives you to succeed in your positions, you must realize an overemphasis in this quadrant can dominate your life so much that the power of the other three quadrants diminishes. If you are cringing in self-reflection at this point, it might be helpful to note the reasons you tend to focus so hard here. From an early age, we are programmed to focus on our positions:

- What do you want to be when you grow up?
- What is your plan after you graduate?
- What are you majoring in?
- What do you plan to do with your degree?

Add in the financial obligations associated with growing up and developing through the stages of life, and you end up with social pressures, as well as internal pressures, to succeed or exceed in order to prove something or provide financial stability for a family. Reasons for an overemphasis on this quadrant can also stem from pure intentions in education, giving all we have to our students and staff. Regardless of the intention, imbalance stemming from saturation in this quadrant can leave sweeping and dire consequences.

Navigating the Course

Jessica. As a school leader, I am a community builder. Even growing up, I was someone who didn't want anyone sitting alone. As such, I've been challenged to build relationships—while setting boundaries—with others who don't want to get on the proverbial bus when we set our visions for our school. Many times when I need to have a difficult conversation, I reflect on what I want the other person to hear and how I can say things to make the message clear. I try to always have these conversations in person, keep them short, and use as few words as possible to make my point. In my experience, being direct, but sincere, is important to ensure the person hears *my* message (not the "rose-colored glasses" version of it) and has time to process it. For example, when one of my staff members is always late to work, this impacts what I need to do and how the school runs. Which conversation option below do you think would best be heard by the staff member?

"Hey, I am sure you have really good reasons each day for being late."

"I know it is only ten to fifteen minutes and, if we didn't have staff meetings right away, it wouldn't be that big a deal. But, anyway, do you think you could try to be closer to on time?"

or

"Charles, I really enjoy the conversations and ideas you share and how they benefit the school. However, when you are late to work, it impacts those discussions because the rest of us either have to wait until you arrive to start, or your voice isn't heard because you are not present. I will check back with you later on how you are going to start coming to work on time."

See the difference? I have found the second option allows me to be direct but, in my own way, still get the message across. I have also learned that until the other person really understands how their behavior impacts the school and students, they won't change. ■

Regardless of your title, you may find it hard to separate yourself from your position. For example, when delivering a difficult message to a coworker, a student, or a teacher, you can get wrapped up in how the interaction will affect your relationship with them instead of focusing on why the message needs to be given. It is important to always make your decisions based on what is best for students, not just in the classroom, but also in conversations with your colleagues. As hard as it can be at times, when you continue to focus on what is best for students, keeping your decisions professional, it is much easier to go home at night and not let things affect you personally. No matter what colleagues may say, you will sleep better knowing you are doing right by kids.

We advocate for starting each day personally with intentionality and we promote the same practice in your position. Once the school year gets going, days can just fly by and before you know it you've come to the end of a school year exhausted, wishing you would have accomplished more with your students. It's important to schedule in regular time for yourself to reflect on progress throughout the year. Ideally, this would be a school-wide priority with systems in place for reflection (we are familiar with required components that include self-reflection, student surveys, student-learning objective goals, professional-practice goals, etc.), but we know this is not the case in all schools. Whether your school has similar components in place or not, we encourage you not to think of these practices as required "hoops you have to jump through" or tedious paperwork, but rather look at these kind of practices as significant points of the year to hit "pause" to reflect on progress made—in your role and in its impact on students, staff, and community. Taking time to reflect on your impact gives value and purpose to your work. When we feel the urgency of our purpose, it gives meaning to our work. It gives us our "why" each day we walk into the building. It is with this mindset that we get better and better each day in our position, to not only be the best educator we can be, but to impact children the best we can. Isn't that why we are here in this profession?

Jessica. If you're not sure where to start this process, think about your classroom or building goals. If they're like mine, they usually look amazing in August—beautiful fonts, eloquent words. (In fact, at our school, we even sign collective commitments and review them weekly.) But what happens to those goals and plans during the year? Reflect on your own practice. Are you doing in January what you set out to do in July?

Mid-year, I review our site plan. Are we on track to accomplish our goals? If not, what has gotten in the way? What things came up mid-year we didn't expect? What can I do to get us back on course? Taking the time in January—just like in July—to refocus on our goals gives me the strength needed to continue the school year with the purpose and passion I started with in August. ■

In addition to your goals, you may want to spend some time reflecting on your time management. With your current time management/organization processes, are you accomplishing what you need to during the school day? Are you bringing home piles each evening? While there are seasons of the year that the piles tend to get heavier than others (although nowadays it's actually not the heavy bag, it's actually just a ton of digital work), we find time and time again that if we leave it at school and take evening time to recharge, we actually return to work with more energy and a better attitude and can "tackle" the work with much more efficiency than if we were working on it late at night. Are there any areas of your work that could use some "tweaking" to make them more efficient?

While our calling is a critical component to each of us and what we do every day, it is also important to make sure our positional quadrant doesn't become the consistent priority. Setting boundaries between home and school is critical to ensure you have time for the other quadrants and opportunities to balance out aspects in your life. Time management strategies are helpful to help address boundaries and create time for your other life priorities.

Cannonballs to Avoid

Don't become the human porta potty.

Jessica. When I talk with other educators who are frustrated with the "monkeys" other people are throwing at them (thank you, Todd Whitaker, for your incredible resource *Shifting the Monkey*! I just took the analogy up a notch), I caution them about becoming a "human porta potty." I realized I was becoming a human porta potty when I allowed people to walk into my office, dump their problems, wipe their issues away, and grab a shot of hand sanitizer on the way out. Guess what I was left with?? *Their* stuff! ■

You got into education because you wanted to help others—but not at the expense of harming yourself. Once you recognize the people who tend to do the dumping, set boundaries when you interact with them. Sometimes silence is the best option. If someone is always complaining, don't feel the need to comment, solve, or condone. Pretty soon they will realize you aren't the audience for their message and will move on to someone else.

Another "dumping" ground can be created by the people who are always asking, "So what was your email about?" or, "Did I miss anything at the staff meeting?" They are the ones who seem to have difficulty with personal responsibility or want you to make their lives simpler. Don't fall into the trap of taking on this extra work. Direct them back to the resource they're asking about. Give them the opportunity to solve their own problems. For example:

- "Janet, let's head back to your classroom and check your email permissions. I sure wouldn't want important messages going into your junk folder."
- "Ryan, check out the notes from our staff meeting in the Google folder. I will check with you later to see what specific questions you have from the notes and what steps you are going to take on the action items addressed in the 'nuts and bolts' section of the meeting."

Giving guidance and setting boundaries allows you to help others but also gives you permission to step back when they try to put their problems on your plate.

Keep your middle-school girl at bay.

Jessica. As a recovering middle-school assistant principal, I at times revert to the snarky, passive-aggressive, unproductive tone and talk that I was surrounded with in that setting. There are days when certain people's questions, comments, or situations just bring out that middle-school girl reaction in my head. And while using this tone won't build community, establish a positive school culture, or enhance relationships, sometimes it just feels good to say it! To prevent my middle-school girl voice from coming out, I use a tool called the "thought bubble/talk bubble" approach. If I'm frustrated by someone, something, or a situation, I take a moment to write down what I am thinking or *want to say* and then use reframing techniques to create a template of what I *need to say* instead.

Billy Eddy, president of the High Conflict Institute, created the BIFF Framework I use to create professional responses (and honestly, keeps me employed!) to replace the middle-school girl voice in my head. "BIFF" is an acronym for *Brief, Informative, Friendly,* and *Firm* that helps me with my thought bubble/talk bubble process.

Brief: Make sure your response is short and to the point, specific to the situation, and objective.

Informative: Use specific and objective statements. Try not to engage in an argument over someone else's perceptions or feelings.

Friendly: Attempt to find ways to see their perspective and to understand the place they are coming from is good.

Firm: Set a date for a meeting if further discussion is needed, but choose your words well so this does not turn into a debate. Discussion over.

An additional tool I use is the process of "phoning a friend before you hit send." I ask a critical supervisor to review my responses before I send them to ensure they are appropriate and professional. This allows me to get an outside person's perspective as well as give a "head's up" to my superintendent in case the issue rolls her way next. ■

Set Sail

- Are you spending a lot of your family and home time on your positional tasks? What are some boundaries you can define so you are not bringing work home with you?
- List all of the titles/extra duties you hold. Which ones take up the most of your time at work and which drip into other aspects of your life?
- Consider a time when you have felt overwhelmed in your position. Reflect on what was in your control and what was out of your control in that space. What actions could you take or what boundaries could you set to avoid feeling this way in the future? What tweaks could you make in your day-to-day work so you can relax and rejuvenate each evening?

Tweet it out with #BalanceLAP.

PASSIONS

The miracle isn't that I finished. The miracle
is that I had the courage to start.
—John Bingham

You can only become truly accomplished
at something you love. Don't make money
your goal. Instead pursue the things you
love doing and then do them so well that
people can't take their eyes off of you.
—Maya Angelou

When did we decide that work and life were supposed to be focused on job titles and families and forgot to take into account what fuels us as beings? We believe that the best way to continually strive for balance is to keep a focus on what lights us up, our passions.

Dreams. Everyone has them. From a young age you wanted to be a firefighter, teacher, basketball player, rock star, or _____ (fill in the blank). As you have grown up, your dreams have likely changed; however, it is critical to keep them and cultivate them into realities. This is where the passion quadrant comes in. Your passions are what define your true self and what those who know you best see as *you*. Without them, you aren't complete.

Each person has special talents—the things they enjoy doing when they are away from school. Making intentional time to cultivate your dream and following through with courage and discipline is important not only for you, but for the students you serve. So don't hide it from your students! You strive to find out as much as you can about *their* passions, but how often do you share *your* passions with them? George Couros, author of *The Innovator's Mindset,* shares the example of "Identity Day," a school day devoted to students *and* teachers sharing one thing they are passionate about. Since we believe it is important for us to stoke our students' passions, should we not model and lead by example in this as well?

Jessica. During my trip to Washington D.C. to receive the Minnesota National Distinguished Principal Award, I took videos and posted them to our school Facebook page so students could follow my journey. When I returned, students asked about my trip, what I liked best, and asked to see the award. They wanted to know more about me! ◼

We also define this quadrant as the areas of life igniting your soul and bringing out your true self. You can have professional passions as well as personal passions. Even better is when the two collide! And it is important not to allow these passions to die as you prioritize the other quadrants.

Sarah. When I was young, I loved to perform and sing publicly. Until I had children, I fueled this passion through high-school productions, community theater, and being a wedding singer (though not the cool kind like Adam Sandler's character!). However, when personal, professional, and positional priorities took over, suddenly a decade passed without my stoking this flame. Now, with a healthy focus on balance, I am building in little opportunities to share my passion by singing with our choir, performing the national anthem at sporting events, and developing fun skits with our faculty for our student assemblies. Writing is another passion I have long held. In fact, I became an English teacher in small part because of my passion for reading and writing. Seeking balance in this quadrant means composing blog posts and crafting this very text! ∎

Maybe your passion is art, sports, tinkering with electronics, building projects, or comedy. Please do not forget what ignites the passionate flames within you, and take some time to breathe air into those embers. The light within you shines most luminously when the flames of passion burn brightest.

Navigating the Course

Sarah. My young-adult dream was to be an actress. In fact, for my entire senior year, my unrealistic plan was to attend a college in Florida for acting—solely based on a flier they had sent me. I cut out the image of their institution and kept it in my wallet as a reminder and a way to connect with this dream. I was a first-generation college student, as both parents were hard-working people without advanced degrees who loved one another deeply and built a large family of seven children. There was not a lot of emphasis on post-secondary education in my upbringing and very little discussion about pragmatic career skills for the future. But they did attend my plays and take me out for dinner at my favorite restaurant on opening night as well as consistently bring the traditional bouquet of flowers in support after the curtain closed. And there were many of them. Between all the offerings at school and supplementing it with community theater, I seemed always to be in a production of sorts. My dreams were based in what I loved. Singing. Acting. Entertaining masses. Engaging intensely with a group of fellow actors through shared experience and vulnerability in the spotlight. I thrived under the lights of the stage and relished the vantage point from the edge of the curtain where my heart pumped just before taking the step out to the space where hundreds of eyes were focused in that moment on my success or failure. The sheer experience was exhilarating to me, and this was the space from which my flames burned and confidence flowed. But, like a lot of us, my dreams did not seem to easily monetize, and began to look unworthy. The stage was not where my gifts were to funnel. The separation from my passion began with a switch of destination and major.

After a college visit, which I attended with a friend with the absolute base intent of getting out of class, I enrolled myself and selected broadcast journalism as a major. I figured it included the thrill from the pressure to perform as well as writing. What a win! My rationale was that I could always find community theater somewhere. Thus started the trend of being stretched away from my passion for the stage. But I have never fully let it go.

Entering my second year of college, my life was tattered from a life-changing loss of a very close friend to suicide. I was enrolled in an acting class that fall, and it was no surprise that the course aided me through pain. I also met the man who would be my husband that term and began a transformation into the life path designed for me. My dreams of the stage faded as a new dream evolved to become a teacher. In fact, this decision emerged from deep reflection and a calling to use my passions for writing, love of kids, and joy for speaking and listening, as well as performing in a classroom every day! It also melded those passions in a monetized way. Win-win.

My passion for theater and performing arts has never faded, it has simply evolved. Instead of performing on stage myself—though I have done that a few times over the decades—I keep myself balanced by attending shows. One of my favorite memories to make with my daughter is attending shows, both locally performed and professional productions. When I was teaching, a coworker and I collaborated to start a talent show for the middle school. Then I moved it into the high school. Now, it is part of what we do at the end of the school year in my current position. There will always be ways to stoke the flames of this passion that allow me to engage with the internal thrill. Every time a curtain opens, my heart pumps.

Teasing out our passions and using them as gifts in the other spaces of our lives is the optimal goal. While I no longer feel the need to sing/dance (and not well)/read a script on stage, I do love speaking to audiences. The focus is on them now with whatever message they are meant to be receiving that day, and I see these experiences as a calling. Yes, there is always some level of song embedded too, because that is just how I am made. The passion within me for the important messages flowing through me is what makes up the script now. And I am not dependent upon a stage, a spotlight, or another author to deliver the message. I just get to do it daily and sometimes to large audiences. The delivery doesn't have to be grand, and I don't need to orchestrate the performance. The joy is found in immersing myself in my passions, and the best part is that they are at the ready whenever I want to access them. The key is simply not to let them go, remember what it is that makes your own heart pump, and find ways to make that happen. Often. ■

Cannonballs to Avoid

Get a life!

In 2011, I attended a literacy workshop led by Regie Routman, literacy expert and author of several books I had read. I was like a sponge soaking up as much wisdom as I could! Not only did I learn about literacy from her, I also heard a message about life I swear she said just for me. Regie shared how she models writing for students—by writing about life experiences, opening up and sharing stories about herself with her students, as she did with us in the workshop. I was mesmerized as I listened to her connect personal stories to herself as a writer and reader.

Regie emphasized she was able to model herself as a writer because she valued having a life outside of work, giving her stories to write about. She stressed the importance of leaving work at work, and enjoying life. She said if you don't, you don't have any experiences to write about. This was profound as I reflected on my life. I have been a workaholic since my very first job—at age fifteen, when my mom signed a waiver for me to work more than the maximum number of hours allowed at McDonald's. At one point in college, I had three different jobs. Even with my first teaching position, I had an extra job on the side, working evenings and weekends—in addition to the lesson planning and grading work I did even later in the evenings!

As I thought about the personal stories I might share to model writing or connect to learning, I realized I didn't have any. I didn't have a life outside of school! Yes, I'd had many passions and interests when I was younger, but I didn't spend any time on them anymore. I hardly even spent time with my husband, other than watching the same TV show with him at night (while I was multitasking with schoolwork). I left Regie's workshop not only with a wealth of practical knowledge about literacy practices, but with a personal mission to get a life!

I began to read more for pleasure, personal development, and professional growth. For seven years now, I have faithfully kept track of the books I read, and I notice I read fewer books in a year's time when I focus more on nonfiction books. I see this as a reminder I can have a better life as a reader when I read more books for pleasure.

But no matter how much I tried, I couldn't leave work at work. However, I did make it a personal goal only to bring work home two nights a week and one day on the weekend. Plus, I finally took action on my lifelong goal to be an author and actually put time on my calendar to write. And I did! I also connected with other authors and read more to grow as a writer. I even included my oldest son in my endeavor, using his interest in Minecraft to write a youth novel to try to appeal to boys like him who would rather play the game than read. He loved telling me the details I needed to include and even created the picture for the cover of the book.

I added family-fun events—movies, a family 5K race, a day trip to a state park, laser-tag night, or an arcade outing—to our calendar so we would have something fun to look forward to. And I joined my husband in his odd interest (well, I found it odd) in pinball machines, searching online for locations with unique pinball games we hadn't played yet. (Yes, there's actually something like Facebook, just for pinball nerds. But that could become another whole story, and I fear you would all judge me more!) We even took a family trip to a pinball factory to learn how they are made. I also made it a priority to put a weeklong vacation on our family calendar each year.

Each time I pulled off the work "Band-aid" just to relax and enjoy life, I returned to work rejuvenated and with a clear mind, able to be more productive and focused. The "old me" would have stressed over the items I didn't cross off my list and stayed up late to work on them, returning early the following day to keep on going. The "new me" realizes if there isn't a pressing deadline, life goes on if I leave an item on my list. Now I start the next day rested and can accomplish more because I'm not tired and on the verge of burnout. ■

White Space

If your calendar looks more like an all-consuming "to do" list with no pause in the pace of your day, you have an issue. Filling up your schedule with meetings and appointments, and no opportunities to slow down, will eventually catch up with you. The "catching up" could be getting sick, not feeling accomplished, or freaking out (we will define "freaking out" in Section Four). If "white space" is a new concept for you, set aside two (or ten to twenty) minutes in your day for *nothing* on your calendar. If someone else has access to your calendar and you want to make sure these times are blocked, maybe just title these minutes as "Reflection" or "Reading." Creating white space is essential for balance, and the sooner you create this habit of margin in your day, the better your overall outlook will be and the bigger the buffer will be between life and school and your loves at home.

Set Sail

- Open up your calendar and reflect on the follow question: Where might you add margin in your life right now?
- List three activities outside of work you have always wanted to do. Consider how you could add these passions on to your "to-do" list.
- Consider what people have said you are able to do but you have not seen in yourself before. Have people said you are a strong writer? Do they compliment your organization? Maybe they have commented you are a rock star at a sport? What might you be passionate about that you have not explored yet?

Tweet it out with #BalanceLAP.

SECTION THREE
CHART YOUR COURSE

If you do not change
direction, you may end up
where you are heading.
—Lau Tzu

We are all captains of our own ship, and everyone knows that developing a course and a map for a journey is essential to reaching a desired destination. If you choose to take an active role in charting your course and not simply consuming this text as reading material, you will gain an opportunity to take hold of your ship and steer it where you want your vessel to go.

In this section, you will begin to plot out where it is you want to arrive in the space of your choosing. Do you desire to become a more intentional spouse? Are you looking to become better at managing your building or classroom? Are you finally going to dust off that camera lens and begin photography in action? Maybe you will focus on the next step in your professional growth through coursework or authoring a blog. Whatever it is you decide, this section will lead you through the process of identifying those spaces, plotting the points on your map, and anchoring yourself in goals so that you can steer through the course efficiently.

We also acknowledge that there will be rough waters in which you will find it hard to navigate. In this section, we provide tips for overcoming the barriers to reaching the destination as well as stories from other educators who have sailed through stormy waters to learn and grow. By charting a new course, you will be in new waters. It is important to expect challenges. You can overcome them to stay your course or chart another direction. Either way, you have to chart to start!

CLIMB ABOARD

**If it doesn't challenge you—
it certainly won't change you.**
—Fred DeVito

Climb aboard and make sure your bag is packed because here you go! You have made a commitment to do something different. You recognize there may be an aspect of your life you have been neglecting or you want to challenge yourself to do more in a particular area. Charting your course is a way to hold yourself accountable to meet your goals in the different quadrants of balance. In your career, what gets measured gets monitored. So why not use this principle and pour a similar amount of energy into all aspects of your life?

Take a moment right now to assess where you are in each quadrant. This can be accomplished in a variety of ways.

One Word

Take a moment to list every word describing who you are: *mom, husband, teacher, principal, runner, reader, writer, friend, son, daughter, student,* etc. After you create the list, identify which quadrant best fits each word and write each in the appropriate quadrant below.

Ideal Self

Have you always wanted to play the piano? How about digging deeper into an instructional practice? Consider a shelved dream or an action you have been meaning to take, both personally and professionally. Using a different color ink, write these in the appropriate quadrants as well.

Have To's

Your doctor says you have to lose weight, your family needs you home more at night, you are obligated to complete assignments for grad school. Additions like this may be tied to values, but they might also be what you have been putting off related to self-care. Taking care of your health is a *must*—not an option. In a different color, write these in the quadrants as well.

Reclaim

Is there something you used to do that has been lost with the addition of "more" in your life? Did you used to attend church and want to reestablish this practice? Maybe you used to go on dates with your spouse (even before he or she was your spouse!) and want to do it again. Maybe you once found joy in travel but have been too busy to plan a vacation. Write these things in yet another color in the quadrants. This is your chance to reclaim these as your own again.

*For readers uncomfortable with color coding (or lack multiple colors), create your own numbering or symbol system to keep track.

Personal	Professional
Positional	Passions
	#BalanceↆAP

After completing these steps reflect on the following questions:

- Am I missing opportunities to grow in any quadrant?
- Is there one quadrant I would like to focus on more in the next month?
- What activities, if any, in the quadrants can come off?
- What activities would you like to incorporate in the quadrants to enhance your overall happiness and opportunity to grow in each area?
- Is there anything from any quadrant you realize might cause others in your life to question you? Are you prepared to pursue it anyway? (We believe in you!)

Now (drum roll, please), circle *one* thing from each quadrant you want to enhance, improve, or start working on first (yes, we know it's a tough choice). These will be your starting points to develop ANCHOR goals to chart your course.

ANCHOR GOALS

Only I can change my life.
No one can do it for me.
—Carol Burnett

ANCHOR goals increase accountability while providing opportunities to make small steps to success. In order to create a plan, you first need a guidebook. ANCHOR goals are the guidebook and include the following:

Accountability: Who can you share this goal with, and who will help you work toward it?

Needs: What will it take for you to accomplish this goal?

Chart: Chart: How will you track your progress?

Honesty: How can you ensure you are being honest with yourself about your progress?

Obtainable: Are your goals realistic?

Review, revise, and repeat: Have you accomplished your goal? Review your quadrants, choose the next area to revise, and repeat the goal-setting process.

You work to set goals with and expect the best for your students and staff. You need to do the same for yourself. ANCHOR goals are an excellent way to do this. Use this guide as you chart your course.

Anchor Goal
What Is My Goal?
ACCOUNTABILITY: "Whom can I tell?" or "With whom could I share?" How can I hold myself accountable?
NEEDS: What tools, materials, or plan do I need to accomplish this goal?
CHART: How will I document my progress?
HONESTY: What do I need to stay on course? What cannonballs might take me off course?
OBTAINABLE: What is the timeframe to accomplish this goal?
Review, Repeat, Revise Once you successfully complete one round, review your four quadrants, choose the next area of focus, and start the process of goal setting again. #BalanceLAP

While goal setting is important, we caution you not to spend too much time in the details. You can get excited about a goal and easily spend a lot of time planning all the minute, individual steps within the goal to the point you feel exhausted after creating your plan. Megan Hyatt-Miller, cohost of the *Lead to Win* podcast, tells her team to "hold your goals tightly and your strategies loosely." This advice is wise, knowing cannonballs can derail your plan if you don't allow for the flexibility to modify it while on course. So create your anchor goal and be ready to change course, while still focusing on the end destination!

You have your goal, so take action now! Seriously, don't wait to implement your plan. John C. Maxwell says, "The longer you wait to do something you should do now, the greater the odds that you will never actually do it." He named this concept the "Law of Diminishing Intent." Don't let time get in the way between you and your goal. Take your first step now!

Staying the Course

Jessica. Recently I was in a book study with other educators discussing Sarah Knight's book called . . .well . . .*The Life-Changing Magic of Not Giving a F*ck*. (Wow, that was hard to type!) Regardless of the title, the theme of the book was powerful: In order to decrease stress, anxiety, and worry about others and commitments, you have to start saying "no" to them and say "yes" to yourself. Knight shares how adopting this method provided her opportunities to become her true self, able to focus more on people and things actually sparking joy in her.

How many times have you said "yes" to something when you really meant to say "no"? For me, it might be a bake sale (I don't bake—ever. I buy generic cookies!). Maybe you said "yes" to a subcommittee having little to nothing to do with your school or committed to coach, teach, or referee events your children barely participate in, but you will spend the entire day there? Sound familiar?

I started saying "no" to say "yes" because of my husband. He reviewed my schedule and the commitments taking me away from him and the kids at night. Even though it was hard to hear at first, I am glad he said something. Now I could say "no" to nonrequired evening meetings to say "yes" to coaching my son's soccer team. I have said "no" to a girls' trip to say "yes" to a few days with my family after the National Principal Conference and ISTE were held in the same summer. I have also said "no" to different job opportunities because I said "yes" to my family. In the moment it was hard, but looking back, I felt so much better because in the end, my priorities were honored in my decisions.

Sometimes you may not choose "no" for yourself. "No" may come out of nowhere and force itself on you. Thankfully, a "no" can sometimes end up leading to the "yes" you need. ■

JJ. Several years ago I interviewed for what seemed like my dream job—out of the school setting, but supporting principals. Therefore, potentially I would still have a large impact on many students. (By the way, no one at my school knew about this—at least not until now!)

I love leading others, and especially loved a major part of my job would be keeping up on education trends, research, etc. I would get to do lots of reading on the job! In my current job, I do professional reading, keep up on education trends, and plan and lead professional development, but all of this is done at night or on the weekends—after I've caught up on all my other "title" responsibilities. So the idea of an entirely different pace—no late nights and weekends filled with work—was incredibly appealing to me.

When I didn't get the job, I was disappointed. But I wasn't sad about the job; I was sad about not getting a *different pace*. I wanted a less stressful pace. I was tired—no, I was completely exhausted—and I didn't know how I was going to make it long term. But I loved being a principal and selfishly enjoyed trying to make our school the best school for my own children. Plus, I felt my work there was not yet complete; there were more gains I wanted the school to achieve. But I had to figure out a better way.

How can a principal be a great leader and do amazing work, without getting completely burned out? I knew principals who had been in their positions for many years (I'm talking ten years or more) who were doing amazing work, were keeping up, *and* had a life outside of school. I wanted to know their secrets. I wanted to know how *not* to spend every night working on schoolwork until midnight, only to wake up tired, survive on coffee, constantly put others first, sacrifice my own health, and be cranky with my family because I'm wiped out when I'm at home. Getting a "no" to the new position made me realize I could say "yes" to a different approach to my current job (and life!), and I began my new journey to Balance Like a Pirate! ■

Sarah. Sometimes "no" is a result of deep reflection, meditation, and following the course that is meant for you. When I choose to be more engaged and in tune with the white space in my life, clarity comes through in a variety of ways. Recently, I have been heavily focused on my spiritual growth and maturity, spending time in devotion and simply listening for direction. Intentionally creating space for what matters most in life has resulted in a great deal of balance with home and work. However, finding stasis meant I was in a space to transform again. My most recent and significant "no" is the decision to leave my current district—a decision born out of a distinct calling to do so. I am not leaving because of any ill will, burnout, defeat, or lack of enthusiasm. Instead, I am being called to "no" in this season and in this space. But because there is no other job lined up, this is a major risk. However, I am not fearful because I've been intentionally focusing on my children and husband, and answering the fresh call to become the version of myself I am created to be.

I'm confident this "no" is going to lead to significant transformation but, because I have been balancing in all the quadrants and focusing on reflecting, I am ready to embrace whatever process or change is coming. My deepest desire is that this calling will lead me to inspire and multiply other balanced educators who can continue to make broad and important impact on our students, staffs, and communities—and who will seek the "no" to create so many more "yes" decisions! ■

Set Sail

- In what ways would setting boundaries give you white space on your calendar or margin in your day?
- How can you set boundaries within your white space so you don't fill it up with something less important than your own health and wellbeing?

Tweet it out with #BalanceLAP.

WHEN YOU GO OFF COURSE

You may encounter many defeats, but you must not be defeated. In fact, it may be necessary to encounter the defeats, so you can know who you are, what you can rise from, how you can still come out of it.
—Maya Angelou

Congratulations! You've committed to finding balance, you've charted your course, and you've dropped anchor in your goals. You should be readying for smooth sailing, right? Not so fast. Remember the old "sailor's warning" about red skies in the morning? Despite all your planning and good intentions—and even positive progress—sometimes you are still going to veer off course. The alarm didn't go off, the meeting was at 8:00 a.m., your spouse took the car keys, you just realized your kids have a concert this week and they have nothing to wear, or you just completely blew off a meeting. We have all been there, when the wheels fall off the bus, the boiling pot of water overflows, tips over, we consider applying to Starbucks.... The good news is everyone has been there. In your passion to serve others, if you don't remember to take care of yourself, you run the risk of *freaking out*. For some, it tears them apart for days; others can recover in a matter of minutes or hours. Regardless of how you handle your "meltdown" moments, and before we talk about strategies, take a look at the process we call the "Five Steps of Freaking Out."

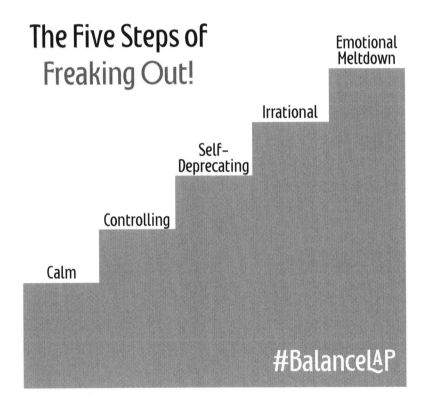

The Five Steps of Freaking Out!

Calm

Controlling

Self-Deprecating

Irrational

Emotional Meltdown

#BalanceLAP

The Five Steps of Freaking Out are triggered by an imbalance in the quadrants. For example, a project at work is consuming all your time, or a family tragedy is taking your focus or joy. Or maybe you're absorbed in something exciting like a trip, a presentation, or training for a race. The Five Steps aren't always triggered by bad things—they are triggered by *too much* of anything. It's also important to note you can go up or down these steps. Jessica tends to start out calm and move *up* the steps to freak out; yet JJ melts down immediately and then works her way *down* to calm.

Calm

This first step is a small hiccup. Maybe your schedule didn't allow you to have the family time you wanted for a few days. Rain, sleet, or snow prevented you from running for a day or two. A response on a project idea hasn't come via email yet. At this step, you are still breathing and still putting one foot in front of the other, but it is just a little harder than it was before.

Controlling

In this step, you start manipulating the odds to be in your favor. What if I just email my boss "proactively" about a timeline? How about micromanaging a meeting down to the specific color and font of the handouts? Or have you ever scheduled massive amounts of appointments on the calendar to keep your mind off the things you are supposed to be focused on? In this stage, you are recognizing something is not right, but not necessarily addressing the problem in the right way. This leads to climbing to the next stage.

Self-Deprecating

At this step, you start to absorb what is happening relative to how terrible you are. When you burn the lasagna (or in my [Jessica's] case, forget to turn the oven on and wonder why I can't smell it an hour later!) or get a rejection from a new position you really wanted—when things don't go the way you planned—you tend to be self-critical, pointing fingers at yourself instead of stepping back and looking at the situation another way. In order to stop yourself from moving on to the next step, you have to really stop, step back, and look at the situation in a more rational way. Isolating yourself and not allowing others into your thoughts and frustration will perpetuate your thoughts and move your actions up to the fifth and final step.

Irrational

Here you are just *done*. You decide you are better off finding a new job—maybe even in a completely different field of work. You take your precious time creating your online job search account, updating your résumé, and maybe even consulting your spouse and your bank account about the possibility of surviving on one income while you figure out what you want to do when you grow up! Or maybe you direct your irrationality toward something completely different than the real concern, deciding the wallpaper in your house is ridiculous and all of your time, energy, and resources need to be redirected into remodeling—the most essential priority you must tackle. (At this point, your kind family members have retreated to another area of the house.)

Emotional Meltdown

And . . . with the seemingly tiniest of triggers . . . you *explode*. You might cry excessively over something small, or snap at a family member and retreat into your bedroom while the rest of the family is still engaged at the dinner table. (However you behave at this step, try to get through it quickly—and with a family and career still intact!)

Jessica. I am the self-proclaimed queen of this step. In high school I literally banged on drums, pianos, or other instruments when I was at my breaking point. In college, I moved into throwing textbooks across the dorm room (well, there was one time in high school I threw my geometry book at my brother! Sorry, Joshua!). You would think as an adult I would have figured out how to self-regulate. But, nope. I completely lose it when I get to this stage, and I will do one of the following:

- Throw a pen
- Throw a shoe
- Yell at the steering wheel of my car
- Play music extremely loud
- Roll my eyes, sigh way too loudly, or engage in any other fourteen-year-old-girl-type behavior
- All of the above, in a random sequence

I have been through this cycle many times, but my most recent meltdown was not with a crisis at school, an issue at home, or an illness. No, what tipped me right over the edge was a math question in my study guide for the GRE.

I had been running on all cylinders at 110 percent for at least three months. My internal mantra was "Just keep swimming," while others around me were waiting on the pool deck with life jackets, ready to jump in at any moment. I stepped up to *calm* after failing the math practice section of the GRE miserably—zero out of ten miserable! But this wasn't a big deal. I'd try again tomorrow.

Then I moved into *control*. What if I had my cheat sheet right next to me or drilled equations into my head right before I walked in the door? I just needed to practice harder, practice more, sleep less, eat less—something—anything. But this didn't work. Next came shortness of breath and, as my son calls them, the "inner crabbys." I was irritated and agitated for absolutely no reason, and I rose to the *self-deprecating* step. All I heard was: *I am stupid, I will never get into a PhD program, how in the world can I hold a job and not fully understand the importance of the quadratic equation? Seriously, what a terrible person am I to not be able to use this math equation naturally in my daily interactions?*

But wait! It got so much better. I had barely set both feet on the self-deprecating step when I climbed right up to **irrational**. I started researching other programs. If a university was going to make me take the GRE, I didn't want to go to it! I also started cleaning up my résumé. Once everyone knew how badly I did on the math portion of the GRE, I would have to start looking for other jobs. (I dare you to top my irrational thinking!) And what came next? You guessed it! I reached the summit of the full-blown **emotional meltdown**! My eyes started watering, my breath shortened, and if someone had asked me what the weather was like, I would have started wailing! ■

When life gets too big, and you don't slow down, the risk for you to reach the top step is high. But we have good news! We have come up with a few strategies to stop or shorten your ascent (or descent) on the freak-out steps—or at least prevent you from falling off the ledge.

How to Not Fall off the Ledge

- *Take a breath... seriously.* Sometimes all you need to do is stop, take three deep breaths, and come at a problem differently.
- *Get some sleep.* When your stress levels are high, deep sleep is a great opportunity for an extended break, and an opportunity to look at things differently tomorrow.
- *Create some space.* Walk away from the problem—literally. Take a break and do something else. Go for a walk, make dinner, or hold a baby. Taking a brain break can be the best medicine.

- *Write it down.* If you are already up to self-deprecating or irrational thoughts, write them down. Sometimes just putting pen to paper highlights how silly your thoughts are.
- *Lean into your PLN.* When you start to retreat into your thoughts, reach out to a friend. Call someone, text a friend, or reach out to someone via Voxer or direct message a friend on Twitter. Do what you are comfortable with, but having someone in your corner when things are difficult is exactly what you need.
- *Make a plan.* Making a plan or a timeline on the front end is a good investment. For example, when you have a big paper or project due, map out a timeline, including short-term goals, to reach your deadline. I try to work no more than one to two hours at a time before moving to something else.
- *Stay engaged.* While it is easy to have multiple browsers open, avoid the temptation to check the "one" Facebook post, the emails in your inbox, or answer "one" phone call. During your dedicated time, stay focused. Do the one thing you planned, and do it well.

Transitioning from a Difficult Time into a "New Normal"

Spoiler alert: Sometimes life at home will be too big and too hard not to bring into the school day. Leaving in your car a fight with your son about snow pants is easy. But losing a close family member, going through a divorce, or battling a chronic illness is not going to wait in the car until you get back in at the end of the day.

Recognizing the signs of fatigue and frantic despair in yourself is important. But you also need to be on the lookout for those signs in others. After an interaction with another teacher or your leader, have you ever thought, "Wow, they are irritable today!" or, "What is wrong with them?" When those questions creep into your head, take time to sit with the person and listen to them. What is happening in their lives might change who you thought they were. Everyone has signs and symptoms of tipping over, but they look different in each person. If a dark cloud is following you and you can't seem to crawl out of the pit of your life circumstances, please reach out. Talk with a friend, seek professional help, or ask your supervisor for resources, time, or other support.

Jessica. I have had moments during my life dramatically affecting my personality and how I might handle situations. Thankfully, I have been blessed to have an incredible network of coworkers who not only recognize something is wrong, but they take time to find out what it is and push to make sure I have the help and support needed.

Everyone has experienced loss or something not going according to plan. Educators tend to wear their hearts on their sleeves and be more vulnerable as they pick back up after a loss, but it can still be extremely difficult. Learning how to move forward after an incomprehensible loss is critical—not just for yourself but also for your family, your coworkers, and your students.

During a tremendously unexpected and sad loss in my personal life, I began to call the transitional time after the loss a "new normal." I had to accept my life wasn't going to be the same as it had been before—I was never going back to normal. In the meantime, I would have to learn how to live in this, my new normal. Much of what I learned and practiced during this time is included in the chart below.

Transitioning from a Difficult Time into a "New Normal"		
Give yourself grace.	Lean in to what you do well.	Recognize eighty percent might be your best for a while.
Temporary immunity, exemption, and/or reprieve. When difficult things happen in your personal or professional life, it is not only okay—but necessary—to take a break. Remember: Your personal expectations of yourself are always higher than what others expect of you—especially during a difficult season.	Pour yourself into things you are good at to build your confidence again. Rebuild your strength and confidence by restarting the routines of things you enjoy and do well. Ease back in by completing the simple tasks requiring little brainpower. Crossing small things off your list can build a sense of accomplishment.	Climbing out of a valley can be exhausting. Give yourself a chance to breathe. Don't expect to be one hundred percent for a while. Recognize you will have hills and valleys moving forward in this new normal.
Examples:		
• Sleep—eat—exercise. • Don't recommit to the "extras" right away. • Find a friend to confide in.	• Morning greetings with students. • Notes to staff. • Organize or coordinate an event. • Do simple tasks like cleaning out your desk or deleting junk mail in your inbox.	Start of each day: • List three things you are looking forward to doing. End of each day: • List three things you accomplished. (Not necessarily the same as the morning). After ten days, reflect on the following: I never thought I would have been able to _____.

Keeping up with All the "Stuff"

JJ. Our to-do lists are never ending. I have utilized snow days—trudging into work through the inclement weather—to take advantage of the empty building and catch up on work. But I never fully caught up. I'm convinced if time stopped just so I could catch up, I still would never fully catch up. Have you had similar thoughts? You're not alone. The truth is, the workload is never going to lessen. The good news is I have found a system helping me stay on top of things better, eliminate the piles and clutter stressing me out, and I now feel much more sane about everything I have to do.

When I read David Allen's book, *Getting Things Done: The Art of Stress-Free Productivity*, I knew I had found the best system for me to organize and manage my time so I have more time to be in classrooms (which I wrote about in *The Coach Approach to School Leadership*). I'm sold on the system he teaches—I've reread Allen's book, listened to his podcasts, and subscribed to his monthly email newsletters—because my to-do list will never decrease, but his system helps me feel less stressed about it.

Before sharing his system with you, I'd like you to take a moment to think about your current system of keeping track of all you have to do. Prior to reading Allen's book, my system was a paper calendar, a clipboard I carried around with me each day, and a plethora of sticky notes covering my desk and computer monitor. I thought it worked. My list was right in front of me, and I could usually find the right color sticky note I was looking for (just like I usually knew which stack of paperwork on my desk had the important piece of paper I needed to sign and return to the district office).

But this system failed when the sticky notes fell behind my desk, got tossed by mistake, and filled my desk with clutter. At home I struggled to be present with my family because my head was filled with items I needed to remember for the next day. I could never shut my brain off. I confess: At one point in my career, I was adamant an evening glass of wine was an absolute necessity for shutting down my work brain so I could relax and go to bed. (Let me be clear: Drinking wine at night is okay and I enjoy it. Being dependent on it is concerning.)

David Allen says using your mind to keep track of what you have to do is a problem because your head is a "really crappy office." You may see this evidenced when you make a quick run to the grocery store to get bread, coming home with a dozen items—but *not* bread! Allen is well known for saying, "Your mind is for having ideas, not for hanging on to them." So the first step of his system is to declutter your mind by doing a "mind dump." Take two to ten minutes to write down every "to do" you have in your head—things you should do today, this week, or this month. Try this right now. Put the book down, set a timer, and empty your mind.

How do you feel? Usually, this activity brings stress relief—the way decluttering a closet or cleaning your kitchen leaves you feeling. Nothing has changed with your to-do list; you just feel better because it is out of your head. You feel more control over what has been hijacking your mental space. Allen describes having a "mind like water," a martial-arts phrase referring to a "mental and emotional state of having a clear head so you are able to be present in the moment and give each task the necessary attention it deserves." Allen explains even though you always say you need more time, what you actually need is the mental space to be present. (I know what you're thinking! When I heard him say this I thought, *what a bunch of BS—I absolutely need more time!*)

But as I listened to his explanation, it made sense. He says you don't need time to have an idea, be strategic, or be loving with your family. You need to be present, be in the moment, and have your mind truly focused on those things when you need to be. This takes a clear mind, not extra time. If you still think this sounds like a crock, Google David Allen, and you'll find he has not only published several books on productivity, but has coached many individuals—a number are top movie directors, musicians, actors, and CEOs—who are highly successful and more productive due to implementing the system he teaches. ▪

Allen's system follows a four-step cycle:

Capture

This is the mind dump you just completed. Capture everything cluttering your head: your to-do's, ideas, recurring tasks, etc. While this is a one-time task you're doing now as you read, the step of capturing happens whenever any new task or idea enters your brain. There is no must-use tool or app for this—the key is it must be handy and easy to use. You must get things out of your brain right away and never say, "I'll add it to my list later" (because you'll probably forget!).

Clarify

Turns your to-do list into actionable items. You will eventually get into the habit of doing this when you are *capturing* thoughts in the future. Instead of writing "secretary," you'll write the actionable step, "Talk to secretary about revising attendance letter." Or for larger tasks, instead of "PD day," you'll write the actionable steps needed for this activity: "Review staff survey from last PD day, meet with literacy leadership team to discuss needs, identify objectives for PD day . . . " This step is very much like writing a clear objective for a lesson.

Allen also preaches the "two-minute rule" as part of this step, which states: If the task will take you two minutes, do it *now*. He says in a high-email environment, thirty to forty percent of actionable emails have less than a two-minute turnaround. Taking care of these is almost quicker than putting them on your list! I also preach this rule to my kids at home to help eliminate the clutter of toys and other junk accumulating around our house!

Organize

Organize all your actionable items in a way that makes sense to you, with reminders and set-up notifications on autopilot so your brain doesn't have to hold them. Again, you can use whatever tools you want here. JJ utilizes Evernote for her to-do lists and Google Calendar to schedule them, and utilizes the reminder features. When the reminder pops up on her iPad, it's like her personal assistant telling her to get her stuff done!

Reflect

Review your to-do list(s) regularly. Take the last ten minutes of each day to reflect on your day and move any uncompleted items to tomorrow (or even further in the future). Instead of taking work home to finish, modify tomorrow's calendar to include the uncompleted work you've added and leave it there. Go home and refresh so you can come back ready to get it done tomorrow.

Don't just take it from us. There are plenty of you out there who have strategies to use when it comes to getting back on course. Check out these stories from our colleagues!

Treasures from the Deep

I found myself feeling like I was a number, and all the hard work I was doing wasn't being recognized. I had worked in the same district for eighteen years and realized at one point I had become very unhealthy, physically and emotionally, due to the needs of my students and the high demands I had put on myself. I hadn't realized how depressed or lost I had become until I made the difficult decision to move to another district. I learned from this if I don't take care of myself first, my family—and even my professional family—suffers. Switching districts allowed me more time to connect with my children and has given me the balance I need. I've learned not to look back, but to move forward and with good intent. I don't need the recognition or praise I felt was lacking because I am doing what I love and it fulfills me. I was looking for praise in the wrong places. My family, my faith, and friends are my foundation and give me the praise I need!

—Courtney McCartney

At one point in my career, someone at our school launched an online petition against me. This document was sent to every family at the school and accused me of all sorts of wrongdoing. This happened over the summer, so some of the folks I would normally draw support from were not around for me to lean on. I felt pretty awful, but I tried to keep a brave face at work. My husband caught me, two evenings in a row, sitting sadly in front of the television with a glass of wine in my hand. He basically told me I was not going to let this experience define my work as a principal, a role I had wanted for so long. His tough words broke through my depression, and I started to move again. I returned to work and told folks we were going to get through this. The school year turned out to be my best year ever as a school leader, and I found myself also creating a greater balance between home and school. Nothing is ever perfect but, during those tough days, I learned I can pull myself back from true despair. From this experience, I know so much more about the balance scale tipping and possibly even some table turning, too.

—Colin Hogan, head of school,
Learning Community Charter School

My teen daughter was having a tough time personally, but I was not giving her the attention she needed and deserved because I was trying to get more work done. I realized this was not a balanced way of living, and it could be detrimental to her. Once I realized this, I instantly changed and left work at school. My family deserved my attention in the evening. Now, whatever doesn't get done at school just has to wait. It can be hard to leave it, but, by making this change, I am definitely a better teacher. I come in each day more rested and confident, which means better learning in my classroom and happier students!

—Jennifer Shaw, elementary music teacher

Before my children were able to drive, I worked too many hours with school and then spent the rest of my time driving them to activities. I didn't do anything for myself. I was gaining weight and was out of shape. I knew I needed to fix my health, both physically and emotionally, or it was going to get bad. I joined Weight Watchers, began to eat right, and found any time I could to work out—usually when I was at a practice with one of my children. I would walk instead of sitting. Those few steps began a way for me to prioritize in my busy life. And once I became healthier, everything in life began to improve, piece by piece.

—Heidi Armentrout, middle-school principal

I lived at school. I was there early in the morning, after school, and late at night. Plus, I coached volleyball on the weekends. I realized I felt empty inside. I did not have any interaction with others besides the kids in my classroom or on the court. My boys were at college, and my husband was also very busy at work and coaching. I felt very lonely. I found balance again by intentionally making time for loved ones, friends, and myself. I scheduled dates, activities, outings, visits, runs, dinners, etc. with the people I loved! I don't believe in "there isn't time." Life is nothing but time. I make time for what is important, and I let go of what is not. The letting go was the hardest for me, but it was the most impactful thing I have ever done. I've learned to say "no," and I do *not* have to do everything—only do what will make me feel good. Life truly is what I make it.

—Tammy Ackerson, seventh-grade teacher,
student council advisor

In my second year as principal, I was investing a tremendous amount of time and energy in a very difficult student-family situation. It was weighing on me and others could see it. Fortunately, others spoke up to help me set work boundaries for myself. Once this happened, I began to see more clearly and got some much-needed rest. I rely heavily on prayer and devotion, and it was during this time, I understood rest is a gift from God, and it has to be embraced! I realized I am not benefiting anyone when I am exhausted. Plus, I don't think as clearly. I needed to stop, hit "pause," and find some "margin" time. I knew what I needed to do, but I didn't want to let others down. I had to learn I needed to take care of *me* in order to take care of them.

—Stacey Green, elementary principal

SECTION FOUR
PREPARING FOR STORMY SEAS

Smooth seas do not
make skillful sailors.
—African Proverb

A t this point in the journey to seek balance, you have spent time considering what it means to balance like a pirate, found a direction in which to focus, and mapped out a course toward improving balance. Our sincere hope is that you consider this process as a continuous striving and a cycle of transformation. Maybe you are taking a few months to focus on one quadrant, but you will reach a space of equilibrium and desire to strive further in other spaces. This section is meant to help you weather through those new journeys.

In this section, we offer practical strategies to begin implementing *today* to get you on course for your goals of balance. In this section, you will be introduced to positive psychology research that helps to build a strong structure to carry you through the stormy seas. The following chapters provide an annotated list of strategies that have been proven to work for all of us in each of the balance quadrants. These strategies are meant to be ideas to get you started and a list you can come back to again, so start small and manageable rather than thinking you need to take them all at once.

We are genuinely excited for you to make these preparations and hope you will consider reaching out to us on the #BalanceLAP hashtag so that we can be a part of your journey as well.

BUILD A
BETTER VESSEL

Only when we choose to believe that we live
in a world where challenges can be overcome,
our behavior matters, and change is possible
can we summon all our drive, energy, and
emotional and intellectual resources to
make that change happen.
—Shawn Achor

I'm drowning in the deep end. The wheels fell off the bus. Crap hit the fan. I fell off the wagon. My ship sank. I can't recover from this. No matter what phrase goes through your mind when life—personal or professional—feels at its worst, you're not alone in feeling this way at some point. Those who let these moments of failure define their lives are the ones who burn out and don't recover. But that's not you. You can swim to shore—repair the bus—clean up the mess—climb back on the wagon—steer your ship back on course—and you can most definitely recover. In fact, you can move forward with a better plan than before.

So far on our journey together, we have explored the PIRATE acronym, dug into the quadrants of balance, shared vulnerably about times we found our ships were sinking, and provided you with tools for you to map your own course. In this section, we will equip you with strategies to get your ship back on course when it veers off. But first, we want to focus briefly on an idea foundational to the strategies we're going to share.

Common across all quadrants is your capacity to infuse happiness into each area of your life. Shawn Achor speaks to this in his book *The Happiness Advantage: The Seven Principles of Positive Psychology That Fuel Success and Performance at Work*. If you haven't read it, we highly recommend you pick it up. (And, if the mere suggestion of reading another book stresses you out, start with his TED Talk by the same title!) Looking at the science behind happiness, Achor asserts positive brains have biological advantages over neutral or negative brains. According to him, scientists once thought happiness was genetic, but have since discovered people have far more control over their own emotional well-being than what was previously believed. Today Achor teaches people how to retrain their brains to capitalize on positivity and improve their productivity and performance.

Wait! Simply by being positive, I can be more productive and function better? Sign me up!

Yes! In fact, if you are like us and need quick, yet sustainable, tips to keep you sane, we've listed below Achor's seven scientifically proven ways to build "happiness habits" in your everyday life. Next to each of his tips, we've shared some examples of how these can fit into the balance quadrants. However, you have to identify activities consistent with your passions and prioritize them in your own quadrants.

You will likely find these can fit into multiple quadrants, contributing to your level of joy in different areas of life and helping you thrive.

Meditate.

While you do not need to devote as much time to meditation as a monk sequestered in years of silence, try to remain patient with your mind for a few minutes as you clear yourself of thoughts, picture the sky, focus on the sound of the clock, or even listen to a guided meditation. (JJ likes to compare meditation to restarting a phone or laptop to ensure it works properly.) Research shows regular meditation can permanently rewire the brain to raise levels of happiness, lower stress, and even improve immune function.

Find something to look forward to.

While you know the activities you enjoy, you may have also noticed you get just as much joy from anticipating an event. (Ask any kid counting down the days until Christmas!) Simply putting an event on your calendar can boost your level of happiness as you anticipate it—especially if it is something you are really passionate about.

Commit conscious acts of kindness.

When you commit acts of kindness, you "fill buckets" of others while also filling your own bucket. Write a card to a colleague or sneak surprise treats into your colleagues' mailboxes just because.

Infuse positivity into your surroundings.

Your physical environment can have an impact on your mindset and sense of well-being. Buy fresh flowers to brighten your office/classroom or add a framed inspirational quote to your wall.

Exercise.

Pretty sure we don't need to speak to the benefits of exercise. We all know it's good for us; the barrier is making it a priority. If you find it hard to fit in, then simply take a walk during your lunch break.

Spend money, but not on stuff.

Studies have found people benefit from the positive feelings generated by purchasing gifts for others or feel more pleasure when spending money to participate in an activity or event than if they purchase material objects.

Exercise a signature strength.

Everyone has a skill or a strength. Make time to use yours and reap the rewards of the positivity you feel doing what you love.

Each of the following chapters includes tips we've picked up as we've "walked the plank" of our own balance quadrants. And, because the quadrants of life tend to blend together at times, you will likely be able to use some of these ideas across the quadrants. We hope these serve as a blueprint you can work from as you build a better vessel in each quadrant of your life and prepare to "set sail."

PERSONAL

Those who feel satisfied with their
personal lives are more satisfied with
their careers and perform better.
—Michael Hyatt

As you've picked up throughout this book, all three of us have faced consequences of imbalance in our *personal* quadrant, and we're sure if you are like every other busy educator, you can surely relate. Thankfully, we have gone beyond surviving and moved on to thriving and hope some of these tips we've learned will help you bring balance to *your* personal quadrant.

Make a calendar and stick to it.

Saying "yes" is easy—then you look at your calendar and find you have no time left for your family or yourself. Fill out a monthly calendar in advance so you can *see* all of your commitments coming up in the next month. Try to limit nonfamily evening events (school-board meeting, dinner with a friend, YMCA-board meeting, etc.) to one per week or create your own needed "rule." Once you have a limit in place, it is much easier to say "no" to other requests that have previously been filling up your calendar and taking you away from family time.

Find activities you all enjoy.

Once you calendar in your family time, you will need to figure out what to do with the time. If you haven't prioritized family time, this may take time to evolve, but here are a few of the things that you may enjoy with your family once you start saying "no" in order to say "yes" to your family:

Family read-aloud

Despite how "uncool" it may seem, children are never too old to be read to. If this is a practice that fell by the wayside once your children started reading independently, we challenge you to bring it back. Find a book that you will all be interested in, like the original book for an upcoming movie or a book with a setting of your planned vacation. You would be surprised by how many good conversations to instill values can come from what you have read together. If you need book suggestions, we suggest turning to nerdybookclub.wordpress.com led by Donalyn Miller (@Donalynbooks) and Colby Sharp (@colbysharp) or going straight to Todd Nesloney (@TechNinjaTodd) or Brad Gustafson (@GustafsonBrad) for "dude-approved" books.

Game night

Who doesn't love a good card or board game? Here is another great opportunity to practice a variety of skills, like math in Yahtzee, strategy in chess, patience in Operation, or just laughing hysterically while playing Telestrations. Declare one night of the week board game night, letting your kids pick a different game each night and before you know it, they'll be looking forward to that day of the week. A bonus is this makes birthday and Christmas presents easy, because you'll want to add to your family game collection.

Walking the dog

Whether this is a family activity or just you and your spouse, taking your furry family member for a walk is great exercise for all involved and provides a great opportunity for you to debrief on your day together. If your kids are like most who say they did "nothing" at school today, sometimes they may just open up a little while taking a walk with you at the end of the day.

List of mini-vacations

Keep a family list on your fridge (or similar visible place) that includes places your family can travel to on the weekend for a quick day trip (e.g., movie theater, state park, beach, museum, arcade, favorite restaurant) and commit to getting out with your family at least once a month. Include your family in adding to the list and deciding where to go. Again, the anticipation of upcoming family events can build just as much joy as actually making the trip.

Device-free evenings

If you have a child (or spouse) who seems to prefer their tablet/phone over the rest of the world, then you will enjoy a device-free evening. Caution: It will be painful at first ("But *why*, Mom?!"), although if you substitute with board game night, an evening outing, or something else your family enjoys together, before you know it, everyone in your house will be looking forward to this time together, whether they admit it or not! By removing device distraction, you can make more time together.

Reflect on family memories.

Spend time together reflecting on family memories and anticipate more to come. Some ideas for this include:

Memory box

Create a special box to hold family memories for the year. After special family moments together, take time to jot them down and put them in the box, and then enjoy reviewing them together on New Year's Eve.

Photo album

Whether you create a physical album/scrapbook or digital, you can enjoy the conversations that come out of deciding which pictures should be on each page of the events you shared together.

Parent journal

Remember the baby book you kept for your child's first year of life? Why not keep a journal for each child to continue documenting their growth in your eyes?

Notes to your spouse

If you know it's going to be a long week (think parent-teacher conference week), send your spouse a card in the mail to show you're thinking of him/her. Taking a moment to send a note lets your spouse know you appreciate him helping out at home during this crazy time of year and will help you to feel less guilty about having to work more or travel.

Jump into their interests

Committing to an activity your child really enjoys is totally worth the time you invest. While you might not have any experience in your child's current sport or hobby, you likely have enough leadership skills to jump in to assist the head coach with practices or volunteer for tasks on the sidelines during the game. You would be amazed at how much more enjoyable it is to watch a game (in any sport), because you've learned more while helping out. While you are showing your child interest in their desired activity, you will also feel you have added value from your contribution to the team/group.

Five-minute rule

A simple, yet great way to recover from failure is to follow the five-minute rule. In his book *The Miracle Morning*, Hal Elrod explains the five-minute rule as giving yourself five minutes to feel all of the emotions causing you to feel angry, hurt, or upset about a situation. But after five minutes, you are done. You move on because you can't change what happened, and it does no good to spend time wallowing in negative emotions. Accept it and move on. This is easier said than done, but the more you practice, the better you will get. Plus, freeing yourself from exhausting emotions feels great!

Date your family

Whether you go out one evening a month with your spouse or share separate dates with children, scheduling one-on-one time is a must. Start intentional "date days" with your children—time that you and your spouse each take one child for the day or evening. It will be incredible. Even if you feel you already have quality family time in your calendar, nothing compares to one-on-one time with these little people you are raising.

Don't forget extended family

Make time outside of the holidays to see your family, both immediate and extended. Whether you have a small or a large family, getting together for a picnic, a camping trip, or just a backyard barbecue will be memories made together.

Make time for self care.

As you're scheduling personal time on the calendar, be sure to make time for you.

Commit to exercise

Whether you go to the gym, work out with a video in your basement, or walk the dog, put it on your calendar. You are more likely to follow your plan if you schedule it versus just hoping to work out three times a week. Habits are built by repetition, but it takes engaging with a behavior sixty times for it to become a habit. Adding exercise into your calendar may be a way to find personal space until the habit is created—and you can make it stick! Commit to lifting weights, yoga, or walking for a set amount of time.

Find an accountability partner

Committing to exercise is great; having someone to exercise with is better! If you are joining a health club, ask a coworker to meet you there a few days a week. Participate in weekly Fitbit challenges with other educators or friends. They can motivate you to reach your own personal daily step goal and also provide the competition with someone else who might be miles away.

Plan for nutrition

If nutrition is an area lacking for you, take small steps to improve:

- Plan your meals for the week on Sunday.

- Prep items ahead so it's quick and convenient to make healthy meals during the week even when you're busy (i.e., cut up chicken or veggies or prepare bags of ingredients for the crock pot or instant pot).
- Prep healthy snacks so they're quick to grab (instead of the Doritos!) (i.e., prepare individual bags of cut-up fruit or veggies). Take it a step further to ensure healthier options by simply leaving stocks of almonds, granola bars, and string cheese at school.
- Try one new healthy recipe a week (you're bound to find something that looks good on Pinterest!).
- Invite your family on a mission to create something healthy and tasty.

Don't forget to see the doctor

Annual health checkups are critical to maintain your ability to do what you love for a long time. The Centers for Disease Control and Prevention report seventy-five percent of all healthcare costs are attributed to preventable conditions. This means if you just go to your routine checkups, you could be preventing a major health issue down the road. Know what your family history is and make sure to get screened for anything that you could be at a higher risk for. History of breast cancer in your family? Then get in for your mammogram! History of colon cancer? Schedule the dreaded colonoscopy! These types of procedures are no comparison to scheduling a vacation day for the spa, but you will regret it tremendously if you find yourself with a condition that could have been caught early on. Your own personal health is a priority. And isn't this why you have sick days? Take one of them *proactively* so you can take less of them reactively.

Batch your weekly plans

While this may not seem like self-care, it is in terms of "mental" self-care. When we are tired, we typically don't make good decisions. In their book *Willpower: Rediscovering the Greatest Human Strength*, Roy Baumeister and John Tierney teach how the amount of decisions you have to make on any given day can deplete you to the point of decision fatigue—when you're low on mental energy. Once you reach this point, you may get cranky, binge on junk food, splurge on purchases, or choose Netflix over a workout (and you're likely too mentally exhausted to think about watching Netflix *while* on the treadmill!). To try to curb decision fatigue, you can take time to plan out anything you can for the week—on Sunday. Look at the school lunch menu to determine which days your kids will have school lunch and which days you need to make their lunch. Check the calendar to see which nights will be homemade suppers and which nights you'll have food on the go during sports outings. Decide which nights you need to pack your gym bag for the next day. Make your mornings easier by planning your clothing attire for the week. To do this, look at your schedule and the weather forecast, then line up each day's outfit in your closet so you don't have to make a decision about what to wear each day. Each morning, you just grab what's already picked out and in the line. What else can *you* plan on Sunday so you don't have to think about it later?

Cultivate morning mindfulness

Think about how you start your day. It can be too easy to roll out of bed after several alarms or check your phone "boss" first thing in the morning. Remember you have the power to set the tone for your day. We've talked about adding in exercise and advocate for adding this in to your morning routine so you won't feel guilty about taking time away from your children to take care of yourself. Want to make time for spirituality? Add in a daily devotional before you check your phone in the morning. This small morning hack can help you to focus on spiritual growth and, as a result, have a significant impact on your mental health each day.

Journal

Taking five to ten minutes every day to journal can lead to high levels of reflection, which is an important part of self-care. (And we promise this isn't being suggested by the former English teacher!) Consider a time and location where you can sit down with a pen and paper and write down your thoughts. You might consider writing after reading, first thing in the morning, or before you go to bed. The mindful practice of journaling generates an incredible amount of power. Committing to this practice can lead to creative outlets, spiritual maturation, therapeutic dumping of negativity, and so much more.

Treasures from the Deep:
A Story of Personal Gratitude

Spike C. Cook, EdD, @drspikecook, principal, Lakeside Middle School, Millville, New Jersey. Author of *Connected Leadership: It's Just a Click Away* and *Breaking Out of Isolation: Becoming a Connected School Leader.* Cohost of the popular *PrincipalPLN* podcast.

In October of 2016, I met with a professional-development coach hired by my district whose job was to assist administrators with their leadership struggles. At the time, I was stressed about everything, and I wasn't grateful for anything!

After listing everything going wrong, I was thrown off by her first question: "So what are you grateful for?" I struggled to remember what gratitude even meant, much less what I was grateful for. I quickly replied, "I am grateful for my kids." She validated my answer but challenged me to look more specifically. I couldn't come up with anything else. The coach talked about sunshine, trees, life, food, someone smiling, showers, etc., and then it hit me! I had so much to be grateful for.

She taught me to make a "gratitude list" and how to incorporate it into a daily morning meditation. She also recommended I read *The Magic* by Rhonda Byrne and apply each of the book's suggestions for a month. This did wonders for my life and my school!

Every day since I met with this coach, I wake up and complete a very basic gratitude list, focusing on five things I am grateful for from the previous day. While this was very difficult in the beginning because I was focusing on the wrong things, this journal has helped me overcome my stress and my anxiety about being a father and a principal.

You can easily start your own daily gratitude practice:

- *Find your time.* Mine is in the morning when I wake up. Yours could be in the evening or maybe even at lunch. Find a time and stick with it.
- *Find your medium.* I use the "Notes" application on my phone and type away. You could use a written journal or even a desktop version. Use whatever works best and is easiest for you.
- *Reflect on the previous day.* Take a few minutes to get centered. I sit in a chair with my device and think about the previous day.
- *Write your gratitude list.* I write five things every day, though some days are more difficult than others. Start with the morning and go through your day sequentially if needed.

Gratitude meditation.

This is the best part of the process for me. While seated in my chair, I take three breaths to become centered. I then look at the list and read it to myself, one item at a time. I then say out loud, "I am grateful for ...." and read the first item on the list. I take a breath and repeat the process with the second item on the list and continue, taking a breath between each item on the list and, after each, I say, "Thank you, thank you, thank you."

This entire activity takes five minutes. There are many variations you can add as long as you stick with the daily practice!

PROFESSIONAL

Live as if you were to die tomorrow.
Learn as if you were to live forever.
—Mahatma Gandhi

Balancing your professional quadrant can include anything from taking additional coursework to simply connecting with another educator to share ideas. Between the three of us, we've tapped into several professional learning opportunities and have shared our favorites below. As we've mentioned previously, how you connect isn't as important as the act of connecting. Educators only grow and improve when they work with others. So find a resource you enjoy and can benefit from!

Consider Post-Secondary Education

Going back to school is a big commitment and can be scary. Take it one step at a time. Look at programs and consider factors that might be important such as traditional instruction models, cohort models, and licenses/degrees of interest to you. Check with your district as well to see if it offers compensation for credits. Make sure you know the details up front: How long will the degree or license take to complete, what is the cost, is it available online or only in person, etc.? Make a spreadsheet comparing this information from various schools to get a total picture before making a decision.

Attend Conferences

When was the last time you attended a professional-development program *outside* your district? Seeking these opportunities is important to gain insights and ideas from others doing the work you are doing. Workshops, annual conferences, or opportunities to participate in ongoing training can be excellent learning experiences. Regardless of the format, challenge yourself to participate in this type of learning occasionally. If you are a connected educator, conferences provide you an opportunity to meet face to face with people you talk with on social media.

Listen to Podcasts

Podcasts are an accessible and engaging way to fuel your professional growth, and there are so many to choose from! Podcasts are easy to add to your schedule because you can pop in your earbuds and listen on your commute, while walking the dog, or while folding laundry. Want to hear from leaders in education? Some of our favorite podcasts include *Better Leaders Better Schools, Kids Deserve It, Principal Center Radio, UnearthEd, Smart Thinking, Principal*

Matters, and the *Principal PLN* podcast (cohosted by our very own Jessica Johnson).

Cultivate a PLN

Finding your people through a network leads to endless benefits. In fact, we found one another on Twitter! Through several resources, you can discover a network of educators to fuel your passions and keep you focused. You can follow hashtags on Twitter you are interested in (find a complete list at cybraryman.com/edhashtags.html) and even participate in scheduled Twitter chats. If you find yourself learning from what someone says, follow them and build your PLN. Once you find a crew, consider deepening the connection and learning with a private messaging app to engage in dialogue. We suggest utilizing the Voxer app for audio or text conversations with one person or a group of people. Some of our favorite hashtags include #LeadLAP, #TLAP, #KidsDeserveIt, #PrincipalsInAction, #JoyfulLeaders, #CoachApproach, #ECEChat, and of course, #BalanceLAP.

Read

Create a list of books you have been meaning to read. Select a designated number, get them in either hard copy, audio version, or on a reader, and commit to reading them within a timeframe. A great way to do this is listening to an audiobook while you exercise! Such a practice is a great way to build up multiple quadrants.

Blog

Send a note of gratitude to a colleague in your school or an educator in your PLN you have grown professionally from. The act of kindness will brighten her day and strengthen your bond.

Connect with Others

Share your professional passions and expertise with others by writing a blog. You will reflect and grow while benefitting others—and it could turn into a book!

Participate in a Mastermind Group

Intentionally committing to, and sometimes financially investing in, your own professional development allows you to dig deeper into aspects of leadership and seek outside advice. Looking into a mastermind group, seeking a leadership or life coach, or creating a leadership book club in your district are ways to learn from and with others. Sharpening your own style while growing alongside others in the same journey offers opportunity to continually find your best self.

POSITIONAL

Never get so busy making a living
you forget to make a life.
—Dolly Parton

In this chapter we're going to offer numerous ideas to tame the all-consuming "beast" of the positional quadrant. Try a couple of these or be inspired to find another solution to bring balance to your positional life.

Social Media Boundaries

Take advice from Cal Newport's book *Deep Work*, and consider charging your phone (with the ringer off) in the bedroom during evening family time. We even learned you can actually *shut off* your phone in a movie theatre, and you know what? You can even *shut off* your phone even if you're *not* in a movie theater. Just do it and see what happens!

Mailbox Hack

Keep a pen in your school mailbox to sort papers and sign what needs to be signed *in the mailroom*. Don't bring those items back to your office; send them to their next destination (field-trip and personal-day approval forms go back in the secretary's box, timesheets get passed on to the district office, etc.).

Ignore the Phone

If in your office working and the phone rings, don't answer it. Unless your secretary tells you that you need to pick it up, let it go to voicemail. If you answer it, nine times out of ten, the call turns into another task interrupting what you were working on. If someone has an emergency, they'll call the secretary, and she'll holler for you!

Clean up Email Subscriptions

Consider using unroll.me to clean up the number of emails coming to your inbox, distracting you from getting things done. In fact, in five minutes, this tool can be used to select forty-eight contacts and newsletters to arrive in one daily "rollup" email and unsubscribe from dozens of others you no longer want to receive emails from. (If this specific resource isn't for you and/or as specific online tools may change over time, there will likely be other options you can choose from.)

Meditate at School

Teach students to practice meditation at the start of each class period, before a test, or right after recess. Join in with them and enjoy a few quiet, calm moments while modeling for them.

Spread Kindness and Joy

As building leaders, we like to spread joy during the twelve days leading up to Christmas, using something different each day (popcorn bar, hot cocoa, jeans day, festive photo booth fun, etc.). But you can do this in other ways and at other times throughout the year. Write a note of gratitude to a colleague or leave a basket of bananas in the lounge, adding to each a handwritten inspiration such as, "You will inspire today!"

Infuse Positivity into Your Day

What can you add to your space to brighten your day? Consider putting pictures of your children on your desk, hanging beautifully framed positive quotes on the wall, or adding a favorite oil or scent to your space.

Give a Gift to a Student in Need

Buy something new for a student in need. Maybe you know a student who would appreciate receiving a new book from their favorite author, or a new pair of shoes, or warm mittens. You'll feel good about giving and will build a stronger bond with the student. Maybe your gift is one of time, where you take a walk together or eat lunch with the student, spend time in his or her classroom, or write a personal note about something you noticed. There are myriad ways to gift students. Start small, and we believe it will build!

Prioritize Your Calendar

Schedule blocks of time for your work priorities (visiting class-rooms, teacher observations, training and staff meetings, etc.). Work with your administrative assistant to calendar sacred time for office work as well. Once the appointments are on your calendar, *keep them.* Otherwise, you'll constantly battle other items competing for your time and, if you do not complete tasks at the office, they will spill into your evening hours, which is time for the other quadrants.

Inbox Zero

Here are some tips to help you conquer your email and strive for an empty inbox daily:

- **Don't browse it.** Email is not like ordering a fancy salad where there are a million ways to approach it. Tackling email the first time is critical. Yes, this means you do *not* scroll and preview email on your phone while walking the school hallways! If you do this, you're likely to miss getting back to something important or an item needing your action. Those emails will just live in your inbox clutter. Set time during the day to specifically read and answer emails. Once you see an item, do something with it—respond, set a date to tackle it, or (gasp!) just delete—to get to Inbox Zero. The goal is to have all emails delegated, deleted, or responded to within a specific timeframe so your inbox is clean and your mind can move on to the next activity of the day.

- **Prioritize email to remind you later.** Theresa Stager (@PrincipalStager) introduced us to Polymail, an "electric boomerang" app. When you receive an email about an upcoming board meeting, for example, where you have to attend or present and don't have to deal with it today, set a future date, hit "send" and—voilà! The email is out of your inbox and reappears when it is time to address the topic. You can also copy and paste emails into calendar appointments or apps like ToDoist or Evernote with reminders to come back to them in a timely fashion, but this keeps them from cluttering up your inbox.

- **Email is a procedure, not an end product.** Email can be a black cloud over a sunshiny day. We used to dread responding to some people and, before Inbox Zero, we might actually lose sleep over an email until we responded the next day. Now with specific times set aside to deal with email, we are addressing it, but we don't worry about it. (Okay, we're not worrying because we can't see it!) And we just deal with it (aka rip it off like a Band-aid).

- **Learn from the "Email Yoda."** We believe Curt Rees is the "Email Yoda." You can learn additional tips on conquering email from him on this *PrincipalPLN* podcast: bit.ly/emailyoda. If you are searching in your podcast app, Curt was on Episode 47 in November 2014.

Passions

Every great dream begins with a dreamer. Always remember, you have within you the strength, the patience, and the passion to reach for the stars to change the world.
—Harriet Tubman

Passion is one great force that unleashes creativity, because if you're passionate about something, then you're more willing to take risks.
—Yo-Yo Ma

A marathon, a book, a new career path, a better sense of balance when it comes to family time, regular date nights—these are just a few of the things the three of us have accomplished this year as a way of prioritizing our Passions in life.

As we have worked to reignite passions we had laid aside, we have experienced not only greater balance in our lives, but also greater joy. If you're struggling to identify your own passions, try one of these suggestions we've picked up along the way—and start dreaming again!

Plan a Vacation

Put a family vacation on the calendar and spend time together researching the area online. This doesn't have to be an elaborate or expensive getaway; it could be a simple camping trip. The goal is you all have something to look forward to.

Get Physical

Are you passionate about a sport? Use it for your exercise. Create a morning yoga club with colleagues and meet together in the gym before school. Play basketball with kids at recess or use your parent-volunteer coach time for exercise while modeling for your children.

Enjoy Entertainment

Subscribe to updates from your favorite band, author, or comedian. Buy tickets to see their show when they'll be near your location.

Get Musical

Join the community band to continue your passion for playing a musical instrument. Have you always wanted to learn how to play the guitar or use your piano for more than a shelf for family photos?

Put it on your calendar and learn. Sign up for music lessons or find YouTube clips to learn how to play on your own.

Find Your Voice

Sing the national anthem at a sporting event. Seriously! If this is too much, join in with the choir from time to time or sing a snappy version of "Happy Birthday" to staff and students.

Develop a Talent

Schedule time to develop a skill you have always wanted to have or to pursue one you had previously. Dance? Piano or guitar? Maybe you want to try a "Paint and Sip" class, or participate in an open-mic slam poetry event. Make a point to get involved with whatever fuels your creative passion.

Get on Stage

Audition for a community theater show! If you loved the stage once, you'll love it again. Take time to do a show and share the experience with family members for bonus points!

Plan a Project

Do you love DIY shows and YouTube videos, but never make the time to complete your own project? Now's the time! Refurbish Grandpa's old chair, redesign your bedroom, create rock or fairy gardens. Whatever lights your passion for using your hands, spend time on it.

Treasures from the Deep:
Tips from the Field

I block off hours for family on weeknights and rarely work on the weekends. If I do work on the weekend, my wife, Miriam, also needs to work so we are both productive and then spend time together. I "batch" three late weeknights so they are consistent, and Miriam and I then have at least two weeknights for us. Even on my late nights, we always "eat" dinner together—about three hours taking our time cooking, enjoying the meal, and connecting—before I go back to work. Our favorite way to connect is through our "Q & A a Day" journal, which has a writing prompt for each day we both respond to. Miriam and I have been adding to this journal for three years, and I suspect this will become a family treasure.

To maintain focus, I use the goal-crusher template I designed, allowing me to align my tasks with three quarterly goals and measure progress toward these goals. I find great satisfaction in seeing my percentage of complete tasks and comparing my performance across weeks. Each twelve weeks, I set new professional and personal goals, and this system allows me to generate a ton of momentum, carrying me into each twelve-week sprint. I consistently reflect on where I'm at in all quadrants and tweak as necessary. My calendar tells me exactly what to do: I block off time for work, for family, and for personal interests. If a task isn't on my calendar, it isn't a priority and doesn't get done.

—Danny "Sunshine" Buer, host of the
Better Leaders Better Schools podcast

I use my whiteboard as a system to track my priorities and goals, color coding tasks as either *important and urgent*, *important but not urgent*, or *not important and not urgent*. I tend to do the easiest tasks first, but I realize those are usually not important or urgent. Using this system pushes me outside my comfort zone to strategically plan and accomplish what helps me reach my learning goals.

—Barbara Bray, creative learning strategist at
Rethinking Learning (barbarabray.net)

The month of May creates unbalance for me every year. The combination of school events and special activities, bringing one school year to a close while planning for the next, and family commitments create stress. To minimize as much stress as possible, I use my electronic calendars to keep me on top of things. I've learned to say "no"—prioritizing what is most important, and I've learned it's okay to ask for help from family, friends, or colleagues—even for something seemingly small. During one particular week when my husband was on a work trip, I was stressed by multiple evening school commitments, as well as needing to care for our dog. Simply asking a friend to take our dog for the week relieved my stress and allowed me to focus on my work priorities.

—Mark French, elementary principal

Google Keep helps to "keep" me organized. Daily priorities are under one Google Keep called "Three Daily Rocks." Unless the building is on fire, nothing else gets added until those three things are done, and I must complete them by the end of the day so I leave feeling a sense of accomplishment.

—Onica L. Mayers, principal

During my first semester, I was hit with a number of tasks all at once and a ton of "new." I was overwhelmed, plus I focused so hard trying to do everything that I made lots of simple mistakes. I was off balance. I had to be reminded to focus on one thing at a time, get it done, and then tackle the next task. Now, I focus on one day at a time—not yesterday or tomorrow. I feel so much more confident, and I've had a great start to the second semester. Here's how I've been able to accomplish living in balance:

- Using Google Keep, each day I make a list of tasks to complete in order to have a great day. This allows me to reflect about my performance at the end of the day.

- I prioritize my professional growth by thinking about what will benefit our students and teachers the most.

- I make time for my personal passions, and I share them with colleagues and highlight them on Twitter.

- When I leave work, I put the phone and computer away to disconnect from the job.

—Don Jeffries, principal, Jefferson City, MO

PROFESSIONAL DEVELOPMENT TO PROMOTE BALANCE

Hopefully you are excited to commit to yourself, your family, your career, and your calling—to achieve balance in all the quadrants of your personal life. We have mentioned previously educators are better when they work together. The three of us are definitely better balanced individuals, in part, because of each other. But we have also discovered balance is valuable—even critical—to our teachers and staff members as a unit, and giving them opportunities to work together on this journey offers success and accountability for everyone.

Jessica. During this journey, I have found intentional ways to share my learning with the staff I have the honor to work alongside each day. Below are some options I have used to integrate the tenets of balance into my school's professional development.

Journaling During Staff Meetings

I offer the first ten minutes of a staff meeting for journaling and reflection. This allows teachers time to regroup and recalibrate after a busy day with students, and focus on the work ahead. Preparing prompts ahead of time is critical to ensure the activity is completed and meaningful for all participants. Some journal prompts I've used include:

- Take ten minutes to jot down one hundred things you love about teaching. Be ready to share ten of your favorites with a table partner.
- How do you build relationships with your students?
- (Pause) and reflect on the good happening at school.
- Write a letter to your younger self. Reflect on things you have learned in your journey and what you wish you had known when you were younger.

Throughout the year, I ask staff to offer ideas and lead the prompts. This is such a powerful way to include staff and offer multiple ways to reflect on our daily learning.

Because I Said I Would

I first heard of "Because I Said I Would" from my #edufriends Lindsy Stumpenhorst @lmstump and Nick Proud @Nick_Proud. This movement (becauseisaidiwould.com) challenges us, not only to make a promise to ourselves or those we love, but to write the promise down, and look to others to hold you accountable to keep it. Two years ago, my promise was to spend more time with my boys. I taped the card with my written promise next to their school pictures by my computer screen and right above my phone. Having this concrete reminder encouraged me to shut down and leave earlier at night so I could be home with them more.

The Steps to Success...

This is, by far, my favorite staff reflection. Using Soul Pancake's YouTube video (bit.ly/soulpancakesteps), I guide my staff through this activity related to their success. First, I ask them to think about the people who have helped them become successful. Second, I ask them to write a letter to one of those people, explaining why the person made an impact on their life. And finally, I challenge staff to call, mail their letter to, or in some other way reach out to the person to share how they were impacted.

Book Studies

Readers are leaders, right? Encouraging the mindset of learning and reading in staff has positive effects on the school community. A few years ago, our staff committed to reading Dr. Adam Saenz's *The Power of a Teacher*. His book is broken into chapters about well-being in the following areas: occupational, emotional, financial, spiritual, and physical. I purchased a book for every staff member who wanted to participate. Once a month, we came together to discuss the questions in the chapter and offer ideas on how we could improve in one of the areas of wellness.

As a school district, we took this to the next level and involved community partners. Each month we offered off-site learning experiences in each of the areas of wellness. For example:

- *Occupational wellness*: At a local coffee shop, an outreach staff member from our local hospital spoke about stress management and gaining margin in your day.
- *Emotional wellness*: At a local art studio, a life coach gave a workshop on journaling and reflecting. Everyone who attended received a journal, pens, and some prompts.
- *Financial wellness*: Our HR director coordinated with local and district financial specialists to give a workshop on

financial planning at three points of a career: entry teachers, mid-career, and retirement planning (teachers in their fifties).

- *Spiritual wellness*: Two local pastors spoke about our calling as educators and how to heal and help our hearts through the rough stuff.

- *Physical wellness*: Local health clubs came to one of the elementary-school gyms and demonstrated equipment, offered discounts on memberships, and a local nutritionist provided healthy snacks for the holidays to all participants.

This professional development opportunity not only enhanced our professional practice, but emphasized that the school (and community) leaders valued every staff member's health and happiness.

EPILOGUE
FINDING YOUR TREASURE

We are at the end of our journey together. We hope you have laughed a bit, agreed with a few of our thoughts, and found some ways to move forward in finding balance in your life. All three of us lose sleep about the fate of education in the United States. We lose sleep about losing *you*, a committed, relentless, and dedicated educator who, at times, is *t-i-r-e-d*. We worry about what happens when your tired leads to burnout—and ditching the profession.

When you set this book down, do not forget to pick your own map up regularly. Do not let the revelations about your *personal, positional, professional,* and *passions* recede back into an afterthought. It is through the striving to be better that we can all achieve greater satisfaction with the one life we are given. Let's all commit to living our legacy intentionally while it is being built.

Our goal for writing *Balance Like a Pirate* was to equip you with tools you can use to achieve balance in your life as a remedy for burnout. Our hope is you will reframe the end of this book as only the beginning of your journey in this work. We encourage you to tweet and post your celebrations, your struggles, and your questions on Twitter with the hashtag #BalanceLAP.

Make reclaiming yourself a priority so you can commit to serving your students and supporting your families in the best way possible.

BIBLIOGRAPHY

Achor, Shawn. *The Happiness Advantage: The Seven Principles of Positive Psychology That Fuel Success and Performance at Work*. New York: Crown Business, 2010.

Allen, David Allen. *Getting Things Done: The Art of Stress-Free Productivity*. New York: Viking Penguin, 2001.

Baumeister, Roy and John Tierney. *Willpower: Rediscovering the Greatest Human Strength*. New York: The Penguin Press, 2011.

"BIFF Response Method." Higher Conflict Institute. Accessed May 15, 2018. highconflictinstitute.com/biff-responses.

Boogren, Tina H. *Supporting Beginning Teachers*. Bloomington, IN: Marzano Research, 2015.

Branch, Gregory F., Eric A. Hanushek, and Steven G. Rivkin. "Estimating the Effect of Leaders on Public Sector Productivity: The Case of School Principals." National Bureau of Economic Research, February 2012, nber.org/papers/w17803.pdf.

Brown, Brené. *Braving the Wilderness*. New York: Random House, 2017.

Brown, Brené. *The Gifts of Imperfection: Let Go of Who You Think You're Supposed to Be and Embrace Who You Are*. Center City, MN: Hazelden, 2010.

Cloud, Dr. Henry. *Boundaries for Leaders: Results, Relationships, and Being Ridiculously in Charge*. New York: HarperCollins, 2013.

"Connecting Care." *Wisconsin School News* (October 2017): 20-21. wasb.org/wp-content/uploads/2017/10/insurance_oct_2017.pdf.

Elrod, Hal. *The Miracle Morning: The Not-So-Obvious Secret Guaranteed to Transform Your Life before 8 AM*. N.p.: Hal Elrod International, Inc., 2017.

Gordon, Jon. *The Carpenter: A Story About the Greatest Success Strategies of All.* N.p.: Wiley, 2014.

Hyatt-Miller, Megan. "How to Nail Your Goals with This Simple Secret." *Michael Hyatt* (blog), May 27, 2016, michaelhyatt.com/the-scourge-of-cynicism.

Khamisa, Natasha, Brian Oldenburg, Karl Peltzer, and Dragan Ilic. "Work Related Stress, Burnout, Job Satisfaction and General Health of Nurses." *International Journal of Environmental Research and Public Health* 12, no. 1 (January 2015): 652-666. ncbi.nlm.nih.gov/pmc/articles/PMC4306884.

Knight, Sarah. *The Life-Changing Magic of Not Giving a F*ck: How to Stop Spending Time You Don't Have with People You Don't Like Doing Things You Don't Want to Do (A No F*ck's Given Guide).* New York: Little, Brown and Company, 2015.

Krantz, David S., PhD, Beverly Thorn, PhD, and Janice Kiecolt-Glaser, PhD. "How Stress Affects Your Health." *American Psychological Association*, 2013, apa.org/helpcenter/stress.aspx.

Maxwell, John C. 2016. "The longer you wait to do something you should do now, the greater the odds that you will never actually do it." August 17, 2016. facebook.com/JohnCMaxwell/posts/10154332611387954.

McGee, Patty. "Help Students Reflect and Set Goals for Powerful Learning." *Corwin Connect*, February 14, 2017, corwin-connect.com/2017/02/help-students-reflect-set-goals-powerful-learning.

Michaels, Jillian. Twitter post. January 10, 2018, 5:00 PM. twitter.com/jillianmichaels/status/951257518432555009.

Murphy, Jerry. "Becoming an Effective Advocate for Contemplative Teaching and Learning." *Garrison Institute* video, 16:31. N.d. garrisoninstitute.org/video/becoming-effective-advocate-contemplative-teaching-learning.

Newport, Cal. *Deep Work: Rules for Focused Success in a Distracted World.* New York: Grand Central Publishing, 2016.

Pieper, Josef. *Leisure: The Basis of Culture.* N.p.: Pantheon Books, Inc., 1952.

Pont, Beatriz, Deborah Nusche, and Hunter Moorman. *Improving School Leadership Volume 1: Policy and Practice.* N.p.: Organisation for Economic and Co-Operational Development, 2008. oecd.org/education/school/44374889.pdf.

"Reported Symptoms or Unhealthy Behaviors Due to Stress among U.S. Adults in 2015." *Statista.* Accessed May 14, 2018. statista.com/statistics/315808/unhealthy-behaviors-and-symptoms-of-stress-in-us-adults.

Robbins, Mel. "How to Stop Screwing Yourself Over." YouTube video, 21:39. June 11, 2011. youtube.com/watch?v=Lp7E973zozc.

Robinson, Viviane. *Student-Centered Leadership.* San Francisco: Jossey-Bass, 2011.

More from

DAVE BURGESS
Consulting, inc.

Since 2012, DBCI has been publishing books that inspire and equip educators to be their best. For more information on our DBCI titles or to purchase bulk orders for your school, district, or book study, visit **DaveBurgessConsulting.com/DBCBooks**.

Lead Like a PIRATE Series

Lead Like a PIRATE
by Shelley Burgess and Beth Houf

Lead with Culture
by Jay Billy

Lead with Literacy
by Mandy Ellis

Teach Like a PIRATE Series

Teach Like a PIRATE by Dave Burgess

eXPlore Like a Pirate by Michael Matera

Learn Like a Pirate by Paul Solarz

Play Like a Pirate by Quinn Rollins

Run Like a Pirate by Adam Welcome

Leadership & School Culture

Culturize by Jimmy Casas

Escaping the School Leader's Dunk Tank
by Rebecca Coda and Rick Jetter

The Innovator's Mindset by George Couros

Kids Deserve It! by Todd Nesloney and Adam Welcome

Let Them Speak by Rebecca Coda and Rick Jetter

The Limitless School by Abe Hege and Adam Dovico

The Pepper Effect by Sean Gaillard

The Principled Principal
by Jeffrey Zoul and Anthony McConnell

The Secret Solution
by Todd Whitaker, Sam Miller, and Ryan Donlan

Start Right Now
by Todd Whitaker, Jeffrey Zoul, and Jimmy Casas

Unmapped Potential by Julie Hasson and Missy Lennard

Your School Rocks by Ryan McLane and Eric Lowe

Technology & Tools

50 Things You can Do with Google Classroom
by Alice Keeler and Libbi Miller

50 Things to Go Further with Google Classroom
by Alice Keeler and Libbi Miller

140 Twitter Tips for Educators
by Brad Currie, Billy Krakower, and Scott Rocco

Code Breaker by Brian Aspinall

Google Apps for Littles by Christine Pinto and Alice Keeler

Master the Media by Julie Smith

Shake Up Learning by Kasey Bell

Social LEADia by Jennifer Casa-Todd

Teaching Math with Google Apps
  by Alice Keeler and Diana Herrington

Teaching Methods & Materials

All 4s and 5s by Andrew Sharos

Ditch That Homework by Matt Miller and Alice Keeler

Ditch That Textbook by Matt Miller

The EduProtocol Field Guide
  by Marlena Hebern and Jon Corippo

Instant Relevance by Denis Sheeran

LAUNCH by John Spencer and A.J. Juliani

Pure Genius by Don Wettrick

Shift This! by Joy Kirr

Spark Learning by Ramsey Musallam

Sparks in the Dark by Travis Crowder and Todd Nesloney

Table Talk Math by John Stevens

The Classroom Chef by John Stevens and Matt Vaudrey

The Wild Card by Hope and Wade King

The Writing on the Classroom Wall by Steve Wyborney

Inspiration, Professional Growth & Personal Development

4 O'Clock Faculty by Rich Czyz

Be REAL by Tara Martin

Be the One for Kids by Ryan Sheehy

The EduNinja Mindset by Jennifer Burdis

How Much Water do We Have? by Pete and Kris Nunweiler

P Is for Pirate by Dave and Shelley Burgess

The Path to Serendipity by Allyson Aspey

Shattering the Perfect Teacher Myth by Aaron Hogan

Stories from Webb by Todd Nesloney

Talk to Me by Kim Bearden

The Zen Teacher by Dan Tricarico

ABOUT THE AUTHORS

Jessica Cabeen is Minnesota's 2017 National Distinguished Principal and the 2016 NAESP/VINCI Digital Leader of Early Learning. Jessica released her first book, *Hacking Early Learning*, in the spring of 2018.

She is a nationally known speaker on topics such as early learning, innovating school practices, PLC implementation, and maintaining balance between school and home. Jessica holds a BA in music therapy from the University of Wisconsin-Eau Claire, an MA in special education from the University of St. Thomas, and principal and director of special education licensures from Hamline University.

When not working at the "happiest place in southeastern Minnesota" or writing with her best friends, she loves living every moment intentionally with Rob, Kenny, and Isaiah.

Connect with Jessica Cabeen:

@jessicacabeen

jessicacabeen.com

Jessica Cabeen

jessicacabeen@gmail.com

Jessica Johnson is an
elementary-school principal and
district assessment coordinator in
Wisconsin and Wisconsin's 2014
National Distinguished Principal.
She has previously taught in
Minnesota, where she earned her
BA at Bemidji State University. She
taught and worked as an instruc-
tional coach and assistant princi-
pal in Arizona, earning her MA at
Arizona State University. Jessica is

also an adjunct professor in the Educational Leadership Department
at Viterbo University.

She is a nationally known speaker on topics she is passionate about,
such as principal productivity, social media, technology and integra-
tion, resilience and the concept of leading with a "Coach Approach"
as an administrator. She is the coauthor of *The Coach Approach to
School Leadership* (ASCD, 2017), *Breaking Out of Isolation: Becoming
a Connected School Leader* (Corwin, 2015), and the children's novel,
Adventures in Blockworld: A Novel for the Young Minecraft Fans. She
co-moderates the #CoachApproach chat on Twitter and also cohosts
the *PrincipalPLN* podcast.

Connect with Jessica Johnson:

 @principalj

 jessica@principalj.net

 PrincipalJ.net

Sarah Johnson has been an educator in northwest Wisconsin since 2003, first as an English teacher, and then as a building principal at all grade levels. She earned her BA in secondary education from the University of Wisconsin-Eau Claire in 2003. In her early years as an educator, she enjoyed the challenge of classroom teaching while also leading the small, rural district in school-improvement efforts and building collaborative leadership as a teacher leader. Sarah earned her MS in educational administration from the University of Wisconsin-Superior in 2007 and is currently enrolled in the educational specialist program at the same institution.

Sarah has been honored to contribute narrative to Peter DeWitt's *Collaborative Leadership: Six Influences That Matter Most* (2016) and Adam Welcome's *Run Like a Pirate* (2018). She also enjoyed sharing her passion for leadership with the *PrincipalPLN* podcast in 2015 as well as the *Better Leaders Better Schools* podcast in 2018.

Sarah seeks balance in her own life by pursuing passions such as running and writing, focusing on family with her two young daughters, and honing leadership skills to be her best in her position and growing professionally. Sarah believes leadership is a calling, and she is proud to answer every day!

Connect with Sarah Johnson:

 @sarahsajohnson

 sarahsajohnson.com

 sarahsajohnson@gmail.com

BR!NG *BALANCE LIKE A PIRATE*
TO YOUR ORGANIZATION OR EVENT!

Keynotes and Workshops

The authors provide high-energy, engaging, interactive, inspiring, and impactful programs that will leave participants more centered in order to lead at home, work, and life.

The sessions below can be presented as a keynote, breakout sessions, or be extended into a full day workshop to transform lives.

- Balance Like a Pirate: Going Beyond Work-Life Balance to Ignite Passion and Thrive as an Educator (*This session can be tailored for all professions, not just educators.*)
- Women Seeking Balance to Thrive in Leadership and Life
- Balance Like a Pirate: Using Tech Efficiently to Help Lead at Home, Work, and Life

Contact the authors to help your educators go beyond work–life balance to ignite passion and thrive today!

Printed in Great Britain
by Amazon